Lost Treasur

Exploration and Pictorial Travel Adventure of Biblical Archaeology

Paul Backholer

Lost Treasures of the Bible
Exploration and Pictorial Travel
Adventure of Biblical Archaeology

UK ISBN 978-1-907066-52-8

British Library Cataloguing In Publication Data.
A Record of this Publication is available in the British Library.

First published in 2017 by ByFaith Media.
This book is also available as an eBook.

www.ByFaith.org

Contents

Contents

The lost treasures of the Bible provide the world with some of the greatest mysteries of history. The ancient Jews of the Kingdoms of Israel and Judah created the most sacred objects ever known to man. Precious amongst their treasure was the Ark of the Covenant, and the hallowed articles of the Temple of Jerusalem made with the gold and silver acquired by King David and Solomon.

According to Scripture there were periods of great prosperity and calamity for the ancient Jewish Kingdoms, as treasure was gained and lost, and the Jewish Temple was plundered multiple times.

By the time of Jesus Christ, the Jews had acquired enough wealth to build one of the largest temples of the Roman age and it was filled with tithes, offerings and unique religious treasures. Herod's Temple in Jerusalem was a marvel of the ancient world, apparelled in religious splendour and devotion. Few had ever seen anything like it before. During the period of the final Roman conquest of Jerusalem, so much wealth had been accumulated by the Jews that an expensive Copper Scroll was engraved, like a treasure map, to enable the re-discovery of the Temple wealth which, it is believed, had been hidden.

Two thousand years later, much of the gold, silver and the precious Jewish religious objects of history have been lost. What happened to the golden riches and religious devotional objects of the ancient Jews? What clues have been left for future generations to follow and where do they lead? When my brother and I began this quest some years ago, we had no idea it would lead to an adventure through many nations.

For us, the lost treasures of the Bible are both archaeological and golden. Many have claimed that the Jewish people were not slaves in Egypt and the exodus did not take place. In this quest, you will discover why we believe there is plenty of evidence that the Hebrew exodus out of Egypt did occur, and consequently, that the Bible's description of the life of Joseph and Moses, and the wealth of ancient Israel and its leaders are also accurate.

The treasures we sought in this pictorial exploration were twofold. First, the lost and forgotten evidence of the Bible's exodus is one of the great treasures of the history of ancient Israel. Secondly, the Ark of the Covenant and the Jewish wealth, first gained by King David and later by his successors, still remains to be traced through history.

Our search was only made possible because of the world's most important religious document. The Bible is the greatest treasure in the world. Throughout Holy Scripture we are given many eye-witness accounts to a lost world of kingdoms and peoples throughout the Middle East. In the sacred writings we have many detailed descriptions of the holy objects of the Temple and the periods in which they became imperilled. What we do not have is a detailed description of their final whereabouts!

Before modern archaeology gained traction, it was the Bible alone which kept alive the memory of many lost civilisations and the peoples of a forgotten age. In fact, it was the accounts stored in Scripture which enabled archaeologists to search for ancient nations and capitals, and from the guidance of Holy Scripture, cities emerged from the sands. Some of the treasures of the Jews were taken as plunder by these ancient peoples and yet some were never found!

Our photographic adventure contained within this book documents our search over several years of research, followed by personal travel, exploration, discovery and our conclusions.

The Search for the Exodus
'For now we see through a glass, darkly'
1 Corinthians 3:12.

The Hebrew Bible is special amongst all ancient literature. When one reads the accounts of other civilisations, for example ancient Egypt, it's derisory to hear the crude propaganda of Ramesses II as 'His majesty' rode victoriously into battle. Only later do we find in the library of the Hittites that this great victory was actually a messy defeat. For Egyptologists, the pyramids of Giza represent one of the colossal achievements of human civilisation. Yet how often do we consider the immense distress of the people who suffered profoundly for the glory and afterlife of a pharaoh? Archaeologists have manoeuvred to inform us that these labourers were not slaves, but well-cared for workers. However, would you like to be taken from your home and told to move immense stones in three month shifts every year, to build a monument to the glory of your national leader?

The Hebrew Bible is incomparable from all other national records of that age. In the Bible the people of Israel are the principal rebels! The heroes are not the kings or leaders, but the suffering prophets. The Bible is unique because it honestly chronicles defeats, disasters and scandals. The leaders of ancient Israel are seen for what they were - adulterers, murderers, rebels and hard-hearted apostates.

The account of ancient Israel's exodus out of Egypt is unequalled in its humanity. The early kings of England falsified records to claim they descended from the royal lineage of King David of Israel; whilst the ancient Israelites passed on a record which declared they were the offspring of slaves! The greatest victory of ancient Israel was the exodus out of Egypt, but the entire story is marred by complaining, idol worship, lack of water, revolts and struggles for leadership which led to a failed coup d'état. At the pinnacle of the story at Mount Sinai, a civil war breaks out. This is hardly a finely composed work of national pride and achievement, in propaganda form.

How very different are the records of ancient Egypt. We often forget the pharaohs had an absolute stranglehold on the recording of history and propaganda was their primary pursuit. We often strip the pharaohs of their humanity and forget they were just people. However, they were not ordinary because many were despotical dictators who could have taught Stalin a lesson about totalitarianism and forced labour. The ancient inscriptions that Egypt contrived always had a specific agenda; they were to glorify the pharaoh, boast of Egypt's military power, prepare for the afterlife and most importantly to keep total control over the nation. Today, only North Korea allows us a glimpse into the real everyday life of the ancient Egyptians. Living here is glorious, because our dictator tells us so.

The records of ancient Israel are the opposite. This people group claimed that God Himself called and delivered them from Egypt for a purpose. To some extent they often had a free press and they recorded their stories in the words of Cromwell 'warts and all.' We learn that Moses was a murderer, Saul was an idol worshipper and David was an adulterer. This unenviable and pitiful list goes on and on. These stories don't make you feel proud, yet there is something deeply reassuring about them. Egypt's records allude to the worst political spin; whilst the Bible reminds us of real life - messy, ugly, sinful and at times shameful. These accounts remind us not of government propaganda, but of the real life stories of people that we know and the scandals of politicians we read about.

There are a tremendous amount of artefacts that illuminate and at times confirm the Bible's stories. However, the further we go back into history, the harder it becomes to find independent confirmation of the veracity of these events. A great deal of our knowledge of ancient Egypt comes from their interminable stone tombs and temples, yet ancient Israel predominantly recorded their history on frail and fugacious perishable material. This fragile collection needed to be replicated in every generation and because of this lack of original records from Israel, many scholars claim that the biblical stories are fictional. Yet, others claim there is a great deal of ancillary evidence to be found. The oldest texts from the Bible, dating to 600 B.C. survived because they were inscribed on silver.

Today the recovery of ancient artefacts is an insistent science trusted to those whose archaeological studies have earned them the privilege of painstaking exploration. However, after an ancient relic has been recovered, first-class archaeologists who examine it can often come to different conclusions to its meaning. Their own studies, culture, beliefs and bias all skew their interpretation of the remnants of antiquity. If you listen to one interpretation, you may believe the case is closed, but then another expert reveals the study has hardly begun. Then we must consider the artefacts that have already been uncovered. What if these represent only two percent of the original total evidence from ancient Egypt? What conclusions would we come to and how accurate would they be?

When we undertook this investigation to search for the exodus and the treasures of the Bible, we knew it would take years of research before we could even consider entering Egypt. My brother and I ended up spending four years deliberating over the best and the worst of the hypotheses concerning the exodus and Israel's lost treasure. We found ourselves studying the works of famous scholars, biblical expositors, scolding critics and amateur eccentrics. In addition, we had to delve into the works of antiquity, as well as studying the established history of ancient Egypt. The task ahead was great indeed, yet we knew we had to approach the quest ahead as TV broadcasters and authors. Our task was not to present a new theory, but to exhibit the very best of over two hundred years of research and thousands of years of history.

Two millennia ago, the world's most famous letter writer suggested 'now we see through a glass, darkly' and his remarks concur with the conundrums of archaeology. We are convinced we understand, yet this blurred reflection of the past still hides a riddle that can confound scholars and challenge sceptics.

To the Greeks this massive statue on the next page was the Colossi of Memnon, a hero of the Trojan War. To the Egyptians it was Amenhotep III, and to many in Rome it was an oracle.

Many scholars believe the Torah was compiled during the Babylonian exile after the fall of Jerusalem and the destruction of the temple in 587 B.C., with various sources over the years providing and updating the text. German scholars introduced the idea that two authors of these texts could be identified, one using the word Yahweh (Lord) and the other Elohim (God). These two authors were identified as J, the German for the Y of Yahweh and E for Elohim. Later analysis presented two other sources, D for Deuteronomy and P for the Priestly source. These theories are constantly debated and updated, also Bible-believing scholars interject with well thought-out objections. For many secular scholars this is the foundation to their interpretation of the Old Testament accounts, therefore they use this cornerstone to dissect the ancient origins of the exodus account.

Some scholars may well treat the Bible as being guilty until proven innocent. You could call it predetermined prejudice. We may even suggest that in some circles it is trendy to be contemptuous of the biblical text. Scepticism can be a comforting friend for a scholar who's afraid to stand out in the crowd for all the wrong reasons.

Sceptical scholars often use a minimalists approach to all things biblical, proposing, "If it's not written on ancient stone, then it's fictional, not historical." Their personal observations skew their conclusions. For some, a distaste of religious literature blinds and consumes their judgments, for others it's just easier to toe the line.

However, for the unaligned they are simply following the reasoning of Thomas. This disciple saw many of the miracles of Jesus with his own eyes; however, he was unable to believe in the resurrected Christ without first seeing and touching Him, John 20:27-29.

It is of course an intensified encounter to see and touch something that confirms the stories of the Bible and many artefacts have been found that illuminate Scripture. We possess Egyptian, Moabite and Assyrian inscriptions that corroborate the Bible. In the British Museum there are many artefacts with a genuine connection to the Bible and many others are found around the world. Some of the most convincing artefacts are: The Cyrus Cylinder, confirming the reason for the Jewish return to the land. The Babylonian Chronicles, dealing with Nebuchadnezzar's siege of Jerusalem. The Black Obelisk showing King Jehu of Israel. Various reliefs of Pharaoh Shishaq's invasion of Judah. The Gezer Calendar, one of the oldest known examples of Hebrew writing; the Moabite Stone mentioning Israel and the Tel Dan Stele which records, 'The House of David.'

However, anything before this time is vigorously contested due to the lack of sources from outside of Scripture. It is also regrettable that the royal archives of ancient Israel have not yet been found; perhaps because the Bible chronicle was all they treasured. Also Jerusalem has been captured forty-four times in history - fire and the elements do not respect papyrus, animal skin or other perishable materials. Yet we were fortunate with the accidental find of the Dead Sea Scrolls from 1947-1956, which demonstrated the authenticity of the Old Testament text. These parchments dating back two millennia certified that the text of twenty centuries ago is identical to the versions we have today. The occasional errors in transcription were so small that there was no dispute on doctrine.

We must remember that the absence of a direct reference to Israel's exodus is not the evidence of absence. The search for biblical archaeology has always been, to some extent, a lottery. Occasionally the lottery pays out a Merneptah Stela - the first reference to ancient Israel outside of the Bible, or a Moabite Stone recording, 'Omri King of Israel.' In addition, we could ask, how many artefacts are now buried irretrievably under the homes of Egyptians?

The Bible's account of the Hebrew exodus out of Egypt is one of the most popular narratives from the ancient world. But is it true? Today, all over the world there are millions of people who by faith declare their trust in the Bible's account. In fact, over fifty percent of the population of earth follows a religion whose Scriptures record the exodus as a historic fact. The story of Joseph, Moses and the Hebrew slaves escaping out of Egypt has entered into legendary status in Western culture. We have films, books, sermons and scientific inquiries. Time and again, new research is carried out, fresh theories are presented and conjecture continues with massive controversy, historical contentions, and archaeological argument.

The Bible story begins with Joseph being sold as a slave into Egypt. After interpreting the dreams of pharaoh, Joseph gets promoted to become Egypt's Prime Minister. Later Joseph's family join him in Egypt. After that generation passes away, a new pharaoh arose who did not know Joseph and he enslaved the Hebrews. Generation after generation of slaves cried out to the God of Abraham, Isaac and Jacob, and He heard their prayers and placed the Hebrew boy Moses into pharaoh's household. When Moses grew up, he protected a Hebrew by killing an Egyptian and was forced to flee to Midian. Forty years later, Moses returns with the call of God and demands that pharaoh should, "Let My people go." After a series of terrible plagues came upon Egypt, pharaoh's hard heart was crushed and the people of Israel left Egypt in one mass exodus. However, on the way out Israel is trapped at the Red Sea, where a great miracle takes place allowing the Hebrews to escape. In the wilderness God made a covenant with Israel and gave Moses the Ten Commandments on Mount Sinai. These events transpired in preparation for the settlement of the Promised Land of Canaan.

Our first step in this inquiry was to consider the date of the exodus. Many scholars who believe in a literal exodus out of Egypt, date it to 1280 B.C., in the reign of Ramesses II. Yet the Scriptures present a timeline that places the exodus over one hundred and fifty years earlier! Almost all the exodus research has focused around the time of Ramesses II; therefore this intriguing foundation of Scripture gave us the synopsis from which to begin our search. 1 Kings 6:1 states that Solomon began building the Jewish temple in the fourth year of his reign, which was 480 years after the exodus took place. Based on the data available most biblical scholars agree that the fourth year of Solomon's reign was 966 B.C. Using this data we can calculate a biblical date for the exodus of 1446 B.C.

Deuteronomy 34:7, Numbers 32:13 and Acts 7:23-30 dictate that Moses was eighty years old at the time of the exodus. Therefore, working back using the genealogies and dates given to us from the Bible, we can discern the biblical era for Moses, Joseph and other biblical characters. As we had a timeline available, we then felt ready to study Egyptian history, knowing from what generation to begin our research. The period the Bible places Joseph, the Hebrew slaves and Moses in Egypt are recorded as Egypt's Middle Kingdom, the Second Intermediate Period and the New Kingdom.

Ancient Egypt and the Bible
'Pharaoh king of Egypt... "You are like a young
lion among the nations and you are like
a monster in the seas" ' Ezekiel 32:2.

For almost two millennia the civilisation of ancient Egypt was lost, consigned to history. The great pharaohs who had made the ancient world tremble were forgotten, hidden and buried deep beneath the sands. Their temples were in ruins, their palaces destroyed and their legacy was trampled by their own posterity. Ancient Egypt, its customs, culture and military might were mainly forgotten - all apart from one most amazing source. The Bible's description of ancient Egypt is overwhelming; referenced in hundreds of places the Scriptures kept alive a perspicacious description of life in this land. As we examined the Bible, it became evident that the people who chronicled these events had intimate knowledge of life in ancient Egypt. Sceptical scholars do indeed search to find their objections, yet over two hundred years of re-discovery of this great age reveals the picture the Bible paints of this nation is authentic, and the legacy the Bible kept alive has now been reclaimed.

The Scriptures indicate that ancient Egypt as a civilisation was far advanced from many others of her age. It was a land of great treasures of gold, silver and precious things, Exodus 3:22, Daniel 11:42, Hebrews 11:26. It explains the Egyptians were skilled in tasks involving great administration and had a highly organised tax system, Genesis 41:34, 47:26. Egyptians were a very religious people, who worshipped many gods and they placed great value on dreams and their interpretations, Genesis 41:8, Exodus 12:12.

The Bible asserts that ancient Egypt was a land of great pomp and ceremony, and could sustain a very large population, Ezekiel 32:12. Some pharaohs are mentioned by name, 1 Kings 11:40, 2 Kings 23:29, and according to Scripture they lived in great palaces, full of precious objects. When these leaders died they were embalmed and put in coffins, Genesis 44:2, 50:2, 3, 11, 26, Amos 3:9. All of this data was coming from the Bible alone, and there's more.

The nation had large harvests with surplus, and they ate a wide ranging diet of bread, cucumbers, fish, melons and onions, Genesis 12:10, Exodus 7:21, Exodus 16:3, Numbers 11:5, 18. They equally suffered from famines, Genesis 41:54. Egypt was in addition a great trading nation using ships to buy spices, expensive clothing, fine linen and they used slaves, Genesis 37:25, 28, Deuteronomy 28:68, 1 Kings 10:28, Proverbs 7:16, Ezekiel 27:7, Hosea 12:1. The Bible is also very detailed about the geography of the land of Egypt. It had rivers, streams, ponds and pools, Exodus 7:19, Isaiah 7:18. Some areas of the land were well-watered, fertile land and others were vast deserts, Genesis 13:10. The borders, the sea, the River Nile and the main highway out of the nation are listed, Exodus 10:14, 19, Exodus 13:17, 2 Chronicles 9:26. In addition, many cities are mentioned by name and some of their sizes: Pi-Ramesses, Heliopolis and the capitals of Memphis and Thebes, Genesis 46:20, Numbers 13:22, Jeremiah 46:25, Ezekiel 30:15-19, Hosea 9:6. The Bible also proclaims the Egyptians were involved with major building projects including great temples (see picture below), which the prophets declared would one-day be destroyed, Exodus 2:23, Jeremiah 42/43, Ezekiel 29:9. Their words came to pass.

The Bible also credits us with knowledge about Egypt's place in the ancient world. Egypt was a superpower and she had a disciplined military structure, with hundreds of war chariots, Exodus 14:17, Isaiah 31:1. Smaller kingdoms looked to Egypt for protection, made peace treaties with her and foreign leaders found asylum there, 1 Kings 3:1, 9:16, 2 Kings 18:21. Finally, Egypt considered Canaan and later Israel as their backyard; they invaded it often, plundering wealth and receiving tributes, 1 Kings 14:25, 2 Chronicles 12:9, 2 Chronicles 36:3, Jeremiah 37:7.

The Pyramids and Abraham

'Now there was a famine in the land and Abram went down to Egypt to dwell there' Genesis 12:10.

The pyramids of Giza are the prime monolithic reminder that thousands of years ago a great civilisation flourished in Egypt. These pyramids are perhaps the pre-eminent image of an age that has both astonished us and left us asking why, when and how?

For almost two thousand years ancient Egypt was buried in the sands of time, forgotten and entombed. However in the Bible their way of life was meticulously recorded, and the stories of ancient Israel's encounters with Egypt and the Egyptians were passed on from generation to generation. For the great patriarchs of the Bible, ancient Egypt was not the story of a lost age, but the reality of the world they lived in. Abraham, Joseph, Moses and many other biblical characters walked the streets of ancient Egypt; they ate its produce, drank from its waters and slept within its borders.

The first question we asked as we saw the pyramids of Giza was, "Did the Hebrew slaves build these?" The answer is, "No." We know this fact

because the pyramids at Giza pre-date all the biblical narratives noting the interaction between Israel and Egypt. It is almost unbelievable, but these wonders of the world were over five hundred years old at the time of Abraham! This intriguing information suggests that visitors to Giza could well be gazing upon the same monuments which were seen by the eyes of Abraham, Joseph, Moses and even a young Jesus!

In 450 B.C., the Greek historian Herodotus at Giza was told, "The Great Pyramid took 400,000 men twenty years to build" in shifts.

Napoleon said to his soldiers in 1798, "From atop these pyramids, forty centuries look down upon you." The Giza plateau is both iconic and mysterious, yet due to the age of this site we knew that our investigation would have to carry on in other areas of Egypt.

Joseph and His Multi-Coloured Coat
'Israel loved Joseph…and he made him a
coat of many colours' Genesis 37:3.

Our search for Joseph began with a tip-off from a Jewish source, who told us it was essential we should visit a tomb at Beni-Hassan. We were informed that inside one of these tombs we could find a drawing of a Semitic man playing a harp - just like the one David played, 2 Samuel 6. After a long train journey, we arrived into what felt like a town in the middle of no-where. It was obvious this place was off the main tourist trail because we found it hard even to find a place to stay. The security in this area also seemed ridiculous. There were two policemen stationed outside of our hotel, who radioed ahead to other officers every time we went out. The next morning, our driver was joined by a policeman and other security men as we headed towards these tombs - we didn't know if they were watching after us, or if they were watching us! The further we drove, the more it felt that we were going back in time, as mud brick homes engulfed us, and the horse and cart became the main means of transport. When we finally came to a stop, we looked up towards the cliffs to see tombs secretly blended into the rock.

Methodically we entered tomb after tomb and abruptly out of the shadows we saw the Semitic depictions we had been looking for.

The scene in front of us was remarkable and showed Semitic men, women and children entering Egypt. These Semitic people were distinctive from the depictions of the Egyptians all around them, for they were drawn uniquely with sharper features. These illustrations serve to illuminate the Bible's account of Joseph, for they prove that Semitic people did indeed wear multi-coloured coats and they show the style of harp that King David played in Israel, 2 Samuel 6.

Scholars tell us this scene shows Semitic traders from Canaan or Syria entering Egypt. However, some people have taken a leap of faith and suggested it could indeed represent the migration of Joseph's family into Egypt. Their case rests on seven clues. 1. The scene dates to the biblical time of Joseph. 2. It shows Semitic people arriving in Egypt. 3. They wear multi-coloured coats. 4. They come from the region that Joseph's family came from. 5. They carry the instrument that the Bible mentions. 6. The text suggests that they serve one God. 7. The last will and testament of the tomb's owner must concern more than dealings with merchants.

This remains a compelling argument. Yet if it is not the case, we can be confident this scene acts as a unique confirmation of the veracity of the physical description of Joseph and his family.

The Famine and Joseph as Prime Minister
'Then pharaoh took his signet ring off his hand
and put it on Joseph's hand...and put a gold
chain around his neck' Genesis 41:42.

The Bible tells us Joseph was sold as a slave into Egypt and a papyrus, number 35, 1445, that now resides in Brooklyn Museum, contains some useful information about Asiatic slaves during this period. It contains at least 95 entries, including names, nationalities and jobs these slaves carried out. The title of one of the slaves is a 'House Servant' - the Bible begins with Joseph as a servant in Potiphar's house then follows his advancement to become the 'Overseer of his House' Genesis 39:4. This papyrus serves as an interesting confirmation of the title and duties of Joseph. Later, after being falsely accused Joseph was sent to prison and it was there that his gift for interpreting dreams opened the door for him to stand before pharaoh to explain the meaning of his dreams. In the British Museum, the Dream Book papyrus explains how important dreams and their interpretations were to ancient Egyptians.

Perhaps one of the most interesting bits of evidence to confirm the rise of Joseph to power is the exact detail the Bible gives us concerning the process of him becoming Prime Minister. Joseph is given the symbols of authority in Egypt - he receives a ring, the royal seal, and he is then given garments of fine linen. Finally, a large gold chain is placed around his neck. In Egypt, this exact process was re-discovered in their art. This indicates that the biblical authors chronicled their records based on real facts; otherwise specific details would have eluded them. Their accounts are based in real history.

As Prime Minister of Egypt, Joseph prepared the nation for seven years of plenty, followed by seven years of famine, Genesis 41. Today we know that ancient Egypt was one of the very few peoples on earth at the time, which had the administrative ability to do such a thing, and the ruins of such storehouses can still be found in Egypt. When Egyptologists first examined the Ramesseum in Thebes, they discovered all the way around the perimeter of the temple, chambers which were used for agricultural surplus, and the first modern explorers called this Joseph's storehouse. One text from over three thousand years ago reads that this temple is, "Supplied with every good thing, with granaries reaching the sky." We now know this temple dates, as the name suggests, to hundreds of years after Joseph. However, it does prove that Egypt had large storehouses, and the ability to hold vast amounts of surplus goods to be distributed as required, just as the Bible describes.

We also learn that ancient Egypt did indeed suffer from prolonged famines and there is a famous text called, 'The Tradition of the Seven Lean Years in Egypt.' In the text pharaoh says, "My heart is heavy over the failure of the Nile floods for the past seven years...there is a shortage of food. The court does not know what to do. The storehouses have been opened, but everything that was in them has been consumed." Many scholars suggest this text does not date to Joseph's time, yet it shares some similarities to the Bible's story, and acts as another confirmation of its plausibility.

We got back into the car at Beni-Hassan and drove for a while into a sand-filled vacuum of a valley, with entrances carved out of the rock on every side. We didn't even know this place existed, yet inside a temple at the top, we found a clue which would lead us to Semitic settlements in what the Bible calls the land of Goshen.

Inside the temple we saw a 3,500 year old inscription of hatred towards a Semitic people group by Pharaoh Hatshepsut. It says, "I have restored that which was ruined. I have raised up that which was gone to pieces, since the Asiatics were in the midst of Avaris of the north and vagabonds were in the midst of them." This inscription marked the continued disgust by the

Egyptians of a Semitic people group who were expelled from the north of Egypt. So who were these Asiatics and vagabonds? We know from the Bible that Semitic people were often considered to be an abomination to the Egyptians, so is this them? Our only option was to try to find ancient Avaris. Then the police who were with us radioed ahead as we drove out of the valley to prepare for our next search.

We spent a long time studying the research of archaeologists to find the modern site for the area of ancient Avaris. After discovering the location now called Tell El-Daba, we hired a driver and got ready to leave. However, during our inquiry we were warned that Avaris is often off limits to the public and the media, therefore our quest could be in vain. But nothing could stop us, so we jumped into a car and left. As we approached the land of Goshen, we had to wait at several police checkpoints for passport inspections and we even had a police escort for a while. After many hours we drove into a village which looked like every other village in Egypt; yet within a few minutes of being there, the local policeman saw us and came waving his hands saying, "No filming. No photo." We knew we were in the right place. The warnings we had received were accurate.

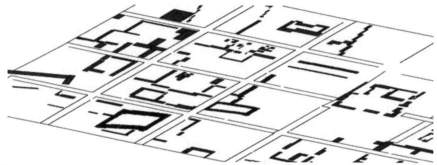

We had nothing but trouble in the area of Avaris; however our extensive research paid off. After years of painstaking excavations,

archaeologists revealed that Avaris was a huge city and the foundations of many structures have been found. The diagrams on this page uncover the foundations of some of these structures. The Semitic people who lived here became powerful and their leaders ruled vast areas of land. In addition, to the amazement of many, several royal seals were found here bearing a name from the Bible - Jacob. The first question archaeologists asked when they unearthed these Semitic settlements was, "Who were these people?" The answer is the people group known as the Hyksos. But who were the Hyksos people and could they be the Hebrews of the Bible?

Who were the Hyksos?
'My father and brothers...have come from the land of Canaan and are now in Goshen' Genesis 47:1.

The ancient city of Avaris is buried under the orders of Egypt's government after every season of excavation; so we knew this area was sensitive and off limits. This helped to explain why we received so much trouble here. As we surveyed the large area, we wondered who were the Hyksos that lived here and could they be the ancient people of Israel?

Egyptologists inform us that the origin of the term 'Hyksos' derives from the Egyptian expression for 'foreign rulers.' The Hyksos were just that. They were Semitic rulers who dominated the north of Egypt during the age the Bible places the Hebrew slaves in Egypt. They lived in settlements which are similar to some later found in ancient Israel, and they were expelled from Egypt in one mass exodus by Pharaoh Ahmose! Our hunt is getting very interesting!

Some people believe the Hyksos are the Hebrew slaves, stating all the similarities and noting that after they left ancient Egypt, they disappeared from history. Whilst others think that the Hebrews lived amongst the Hyksos and it was their departure which explains the beginning of the fierce persecution of the Hebrews by the Egyptians.

Manetho, an ancient Egyptian historian recorded the story of these 'shepherd kings,' and the first century Jewish historian Josephus Flavius, suggests a synchronism between the exodus of the Hyksos and the Hebrew exodus. Today scholars still argue about who the Hyksos were, and to some extent, these Semitic people are still a mysterious people group. At present there is nothing that clearly identifies, or refutes the possibility, of them being ancient Israel.

The Bible specifically mentions ancient Israel built the supply city of Ramesses, and archaeologists studying this area discovered that the cities of Avaris and Ramesses were found in the same area of the Bible's land of Goshen. In fact, the city of Pi-Ramesses was built on top of the ruins of Avaris! Our search here left us with many questions; however there is proof that Semitic people lived here on mass and it is tantalisingly similar to the Bible's account.

Is this the Face of Joseph?
'Pharaoh said to Joseph, "I am pharaoh and
without your consent no man may lift his hand
or foot in all the land of Egypt" ' Genesis 41:44.

In the Bible's land of Goshen, Egyptologists have found evidence which shows that Asiatic people lived in this area, long before the Hyksos period and one excavation was of great interest to us. In one area, archaeologists discovered the buried ruins of a very large building which stood out from all the rest. This house reveals a design that later turned up in ancient Israel, and the size and shape suggests it was occupied by someone of great wealth and power. The ostentatious foundations hint it may have been a palace.

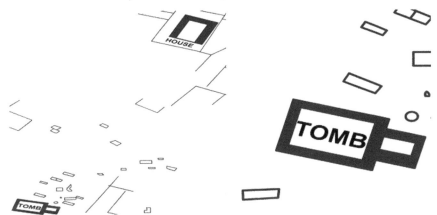

Nearby the archaeologists found a tomb that contained the broken remains of a statue for a leader who was bestowed with great honour in Egypt. This man was mighty in Egypt and he was not an Egyptian! The

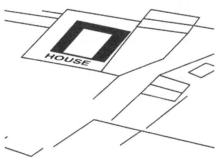

smashed statue was of a Semitic leader, who held the symbols of Egyptian power. He was painted with yellow skin, coloured hair and his coat was multi-coloured! Could this be the tomb of Joseph? It was found in the right place, at the right time and it contained all the facts and symbolism from the Bible. Also there were no bones inside, as expected, Exodus 13:19.

Taking the information available, we re-created the statue head in a computer. By studying the details and comparing his broken features with that of anthropological studies from that time, we were able to begin an artist's impression of the restoration of this statue.

Then we realised we could go further. We began by breaking down the three dimensions of the original statue. Then by equating physical anthropology, as well as cultural and archaeological data, we were able to identify common features from the people of that time, and by matching it with our re-created image; we began the process of facial reconstruction. Finally by comparing the technical details of the statue, we began to restore what this man may have looked like to his contemporaries thousands of years ago.

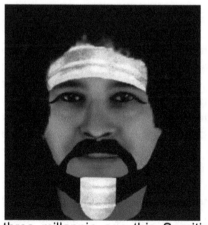

In an excavation in cemeteries F/I, stratum D2, tomb P/19, in the Nile Delta, a broken statue of an Asiatic leader was found. For the first time in thousands of years, we have attempted to reveal his face once again! Scholars can't confirm who he was because there was no inscription in his tomb. However it is striking that a Semitic leader in Egypt emerges in a multi-coloured coat, in the correct place and during the exact time as the Bible's chronicle advocates. Over three millennia ago this Semitic man became powerful in the Bible's land of Goshen. Could he be Joseph? The evidence is compelling, insightful and authentic.

The Lost Years of Moses in Egypt
'When Moses was forty years old, he decided
to visit his fellow Israelites' Acts 7:23.

In our investigation to search for Moses in Egypt, we began by visiting Saqqara the site of Egypt's oldest pyramid. By the time of Moses, Egyptians had abandoned building any more great pyramids, yet Saqqara and Memphis nearby remained as some of the most important

places in ancient Egypt. If Moses learned all the wisdom of Egypt as Acts 7:22 apprises, then feasibly he would have come here. The Bible proclaims that Moses spent forty years in this nation, so what did he do, what did he learn and are there any clues that will help us to understand how this influenced him?

The Bible reveals Moses was adopted into pharaoh's house and as we searched Egyptian records, we discovered this was not the exception to the rule - it was normal practice during this period of Egyptian history. The Amarna Letters show that children from other nations and kingdoms were often brought into pharaoh's house, and given an Egyptian education. The Egyptians did this to spread their influence amongst their neighbours.

On the walls of the temple here, we saw several serpents depicted. It reminded us of the account of Moses making a serpent in the wilderness. Could this have been the image which ancient Israel replicated for God's redemption from the plague?

Our search for Moses took us to many wonderful locations, and one of the most moving experiences was to sail the Nile as the sun was setting. As we sailed, we considered the research we had found about Moses' name. We have always understood the name of Moses from the Hebrew perspective. However, the Bible tells us that pharaoh's daughter, an Egyptian, gave Moses his name, Exodus 2:10. Research into his name concedes something exciting - Moses shared an Egyptian royal name of the New Kingdom! During the period of the Hebrews enslavement and the exodus, five pharaohs ruled who shared a similar name with Moses. Pharaoh Ahmose, Pharaoh Thutmosis I, II, III and IV. When the name of Moses and the names of these pharaohs were translated into English, the spellings varied depending on the scholars, but the root meaning stayed the same. Just as these pharaohs were the children of their gods, so the name of Moses infers that he was a child of Egypt.

We wanted to know more about the life of the privileged in Egypt, so we headed into the tombs of Egypt to learn more about the world into which Moses was raised. The images we saw inside these tombs reveal much about the life and beliefs of ancient Egyptians, and this was the culture Moses was immersed in.

We travelled all over Egypt investigating the hidden years Moses spent in this nation. We've seen and learnt much about the wealth, pomp and magnitude of the civilisation Moses called home for forty years. However, the Bible itself informs us about the most important decision he ever made. Moses could have shared in the wealth of Egypt; yet he turned his back on its great treasures and fame in order to serve his destiny. Moses was not a man seeking riches or power; he was a man of God that abandoned the life of ease and wealth, to suffer with Israel in pursuit of the purposes of God.

One of the cities we visited in our search for Moses was the ancient capital city of Memphis. Noph was the Hebrew name for the Egyptian city of Memphis. It is mentioned several times in the Bible, Jeremiah 2:16; 44:1; 46:14; Ezekiel 30:13, 16 and Hosea 9:6. Isaiah 19:13 declares, "The princes of Memphis are deceived. They have deluded Egypt." Jeremiah 46:19 adds, "For Memphis shall be waste and desolate." Shreds of the city survive in the fragmented open air museum and the statue of Ramesses II lies overthrown by time.

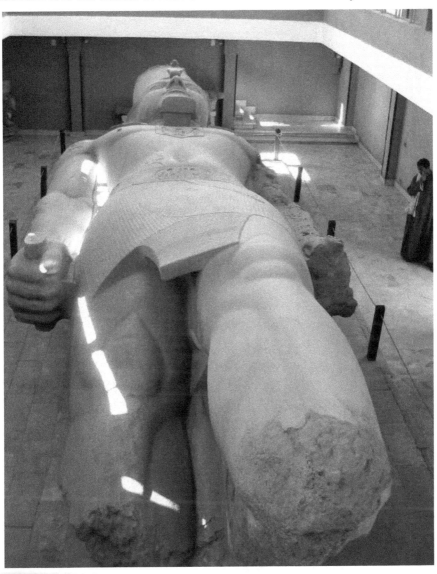

The Bible stresses the Egyptians made the children of Israel serve with rigor and they made their lives bitter with hard bondage - in mortar, in brick, and in all manner of service in the field, Exodus 1:14. Therefore our exploration went on aspiring to locate depictions of Semitic slaves making bricks. We already knew from our research that the best place to look was in the tombs of the Nobles and there is one special tomb that belonged to a leader called Rekhmire.

Rekhmire's tomb is unique in Egypt, for most tombs concern the afterlife, religious beliefs or the glory of the pharaoh; whilst this tomb shows the working life of ancient Egypt. When we entered this tomb, we were struck with how lavish the walls are and the artistic detail. Our aim in the tomb was to find the key to understand how the chief artist of this tomb portrayed Semitic people. This artist gave Egyptians thick dark hair with distinguished features. There are also other distinctive groups, including sub-Saharan Africans.

Then suddenly we received our breakthrough, as we found a depiction of some Semitic people paying tribute. These visitors from Syria gave us the facts we were looking for. We discovered this artist drew Semitic people with sharper features and often with cropped light hair etc,. Then we saw something amazing.

Mirroring the account of the Bible, we found men with Semitic features making bricks, carrying water and doing other menial work. The text on the wall called these people "captives."

Finally we found a tall Egyptian overseeing the work and the text says, "The rod is in my hand, be not idle." In the Bible the children of Israel are beaten for not fulfilling their quotas and are told, "You are idle." Therefore this tomb portrays a unique chronicle of slaves in Egypt making bricks and labouring in various jobs. Many of these slaves bare the features often used for Semitic people, and there is a synchronism between the Bible's description of Israel's treatment and these. The Egyptians may not have told us the nationalities of these slaves; however these depictions date to the right time and bear many unbelievable similarities to the Bible. This evidence acts as another stunning confirmation of the description of Israel's plight.

The Lost City of Pi-Ramesses
'They built for pharaoh supply cities Pithom and Ramesses' Exodus 1:11.

The Bible says that the Hebrews built the city of Ramesses and for hundreds of years Pi-Ramesses, the capital of Ramesses II was identified as this biblical city. One eyewitness account said, "I have reached Pi-Ramesses; it seems like an amazing place, a beautiful area unlike any other." Another eyewitness said, "It is a splendid city without any rival...their storehouses are filled with barley and corn which towers up to the sky." However, the settlement itself vanished thousands of years ago. By the twentieth century almost all the great Egyptian cities had been found, but Pi-Ramesses was still lost and its legend became epic. How did a great city, one of the most spectacular in the ancient world, and home to some 300,000 people disappear without a trace? However, some three thousand years after it vanished from history, a French archaeologist believed he had solved one of the ancient world's greatest mysteries. He claimed to have found the lost city of Pi-Ramesses. However, things were not what they seemed, so we had to go there to investigate.

It took us hours of driving and many police checkpoints to arrive at San El-Hagar, also known as Tanis. The site was far larger than we could have imagined, and what stunned us the most was the fact we were the only visitors in this huge site. When Egyptologists first found Tanis, they became convinced it was the lost city of Pi-Ramesses. Everywhere they found images of Ramesses II, and his royal stamp covered the site. They believed the mystery of the lost city that was mentioned in the Bible had now been solved.

However, as we explored San El-Hagar, it seemed like something was wrong. In every direction we looked, we found broken and mismatched pieces. Something was wrong - what was it?

For decades Egyptologists believed the capital of Ramesses II was found, whilst nagging doubts continued. Then reports came from Qantir, south from this site, suggesting that Pi-Ramesses was there; but how could the city be in two places at once?

After years of research, the answer was finally found. Here on this very location, the city of Pi-Ramesses had truly been found. Ramesses' great city, his temples and statues were all found here.

Yet this is not Pi-Ramesses. The archaeological world was stunned. This is the right city - in the wrong place. Somehow in history, beyond imagination, an entire city had been moved miles and no records of the move exist.
This explains why Tanis felt like a dislocated royal junkyard for the lost cities of Egypt. This is... and is not Pi-Ramesses!

One clue to understanding what happened was the discovery of the broken feet of a statue found many miles south of San-El Hagar, and its other half appeared to be at this site. Finally a team at Qantir began  digging; they carried out a ground penetrating survey looking for the city's foundations and they found them.

Research later uncovered that the branch of the Nile passing Pi-Ramesses had dried up and without water, the city became useless. Therefore the entire city was moved north to a new location and some of the foundations were left behind. As we knew where the real Pi-Ramesses was located, we had to go there. A fourth century pilgrim called Egeria took the same route, so we studied her account. She said, "The city of Ramesses is now open country, without a single habitation, but it is certainly traceable, since it was great in circumference and contained many buildings." Sixteen hundred years later we were following in her footsteps!

Qantir is empty today, there's little to see, for it's mostly fields and new buildings. Archaeologists believe the foundations of the palace of Pharaoh Ramesses II are most probably under the homes of the residents today. Whilst their geophysical survey revealed the city's foundations and a few base monuments remain at ground level. So after thousands of years, the lost city of Pi-Ramesses was found!

For almost two millennia, Ramesses II has been called the exodus pharaoh. However, we've been investigating the mystery of the exodus and we have a suspicion that something is wrong with identifying Ramesses II as the exodus pharaoh. Therefore to scrutinise Ramesses' claim, we entered his temples searching for clues to uncover the truth. Our first stop was Abu-Simbel.

When one of the first modern explorers entered this temple he wrote: 'Early in the morning we were awakened to see the interior of the temple illuminated by the rays of the rising sun...for a few minutes the whole interior was lit up...then the sun rose higher and we were in darkness.' Ramesses II was a great builder and we didn't find any evidence in this temple that ties him to the exodus. So we proceeded onwards, hoping to determine more about him in the Temple of Karnack, in Thebes, many miles to the north.

Ramesses II built many columns in the Great Hypostyle Hall at the Temple of Karnack, but who did the labour? The columns on the next page are the work of skilled men, yet who did the manual labour? We know today that the Egyptians used mud brick ramps to help build structures, as some of their ramps were left behind, and the Bible specifically mentions the Hebrews made mud bricks. So is this the work of the Hebrews? However, the more we looked for the Hebrews in the reign of Ramesses II, the less we found.

We've been searching to find if Ramesses II was the exodus pharaoh and we haven't found any attestation to support this view. In addition, if we take the biblical timeline literally he would have lived over one hundred and fifty years after the exodus took place! If this is the case, why is he often identified as the exodus pharaoh?

As we searched history, we learnt Ramesses II was identified as the pharaoh of the exodus based primarily upon the Bible's use of the name Ramesses. Yet the name Ramesses was in use long before Ramesses II, and the Bible calls the land of Goshen, the land of Ramesses in the time of Joseph. This shows that the author of these passages in the Bible was identifying the ancient land in which the Hebrews lived, with a modern name. In Genesis 23:2, the Bible does the same thing, giving both names. Therefore, instead of the Bible identifying Ramesses II as the exodus pharaoh, it is simply using 'the modern name' of the area at the time, to identify the land in which the Hebrews once lived. If this theory is correct, then there should be evidence for the presence of Semitic people in the area of Pi-Ramesses long before the time of Ramesses II. Then, when we compared notes and maps, we discovered that Pi-Ramesses was built on top of the ruins of the city of Avaris, and Avaris is where we've already found evidence for the presence of Semitic people. Therefore the Bible and ancient Egyptian history agree again.

Using the Scriptures, biblical scholars have been able to date the exodus to the year 1446 B.C. However many sceptical scholars reject the Bible and its timeline, and very few look into this period of history for evidence of the exodus, but we did. So once again, we compared the biblical timeline with the Egyptian timeline and if both timelines are understood correctly, we expected to find two pharaohs occupying the biblical era - one would be the last pharaoh of the oppression whom Moses fled from, the other would be the exodus pharaoh that Moses confronted. Then to our amazement, using Egyptian high chronology, two pharaohs turned up in the right place and at the right time. According to this comparison, Pharaoh Thutmosis III would have been the last pharaoh of the oppression and Amenhotep II would be the exodus pharaoh! We were still inside the Temple of Karnack in ancient Thebes, so our quest was to search for the legacy of Thutmosis III, to discover if he was a wicked despot, as the Bible described of the oppressive pharaoh.

The huge gate on the previous page at the Temple of Karnack, reveals the significance of this ancient complex. Inside the pharaohs competed to leave the most prodigious legacy; yet our interest here was to find information about Thutmosis III - his character, ferocity and lasting legacy.

When we saw the Megiddo War List above, we knew this was the evidence we were hoping for. It contains the account of the invasion of Canaan by Thutmosis III. Every character on the wall represents a leader of a Canaanite city state whom Thutmosis III treated without mercy. In fact, this pharaoh's ferocity was so great that he earned the modern nickname of the Napoleon of Egypt. Thutmosis III led a brutal campaign to wipe out the princes/kings of Canaan and stamped Egypt's authority on the area. Many of the leaders in Canaan were trapped in the biblical city of Megiddo and Thutmosis III boasted its fall was the 'capture of a thousand cities.'

According to a strict interpretation of the biblical timeline and with comparison to the Egyptian timeline, Pharaoh Thutmosis III was the last great pharaoh of the oppression; and the depictions in this temple prove that Thutmosis III is an ideal candidate for the pharaoh of the oppression. Thutmosis III was a cruel pharaoh and if he ruled when Moses was forty, then it could be that Moses fled from him. 'When pharaoh heard of this matter he sought to kill Moses' Exodus 2:14. According to Egyptian history, Thutmosis III also dies just at the time when the Bible indicates Moses is ready to return to Egypt. 'Now the Lord said to Moses, "Go return to Egypt for all the men that sought your life are dead" Exodus 4:19. These comparisons are captivating, as the Bible and Egyptian history find common ground.

The Valley of the Kings & the First-Born Son
"I know that the king of Egypt will not let you go unless a mighty hand compels him" Exodus 3:19.

In the early hours of the morning we awoke to take a hot air balloon over ancient Thebes. From the view we could see the Valley of the Kings below - the most famous burial site on earth. It was the resting place for the pharaohs for hundreds of years and somewhere in the valley the pharaoh of the exodus was buried. But who was he and what will it take for us to find him? In the valley there are sixty-two tombs - which one enshrouded the exodus pharaoh? Once again we turned to the Bible, and this time we had to look beyond the story of the exodus to find the hidden clues and facts we always read, but often overlook. As we searched the biblical text, we found ten clues hidden in the content. For us, these ten clues represented the ten conditions that must be met by any pharaoh to be considered as the biblical pharaoh. The ten clues are as follows: He must come to power before the biblical date for Moses' return to Egypt. He must be preceded by a pharaoh known as a great oppressor. His first-born son must have died and another succeeds him as pharaoh. There must be evidence that he used large numbers of slaves. He must be a great builder, a military man, a powerful charioteer, a cruel and stubborn man, and he must be double-minded at times. Finally, there must be limited military action during his reign due to the losses at the Red Sea. We knew that many of these conditions could apply to several pharaohs, but only one man could meet all! The search was on! Therefore when we landed, we planned our expedition into the Valley of the Kings.

The Valley of the Kings was once again the site of a great archaeological dig, as Egyptologists hoped to find something which was missed by the great British archaeologist Howard Carter, who discovered the intact tomb of Pharaoh Tutankhamen. It was exciting to find archaeologists directing an excavation as they searched for another indescribable treasure of ancient Egypt.

However, we were on a hunt of our own. Using Egyptian high chronology we had discovered that Pharaoh Amenhotep II fits in perfectly with the biblical timeline as a possible exodus pharaoh. This means that this pharaoh has already met a major condition to be considered as the exodus pharaoh. In addition, he was preceded at the exact time in history by a very ferocious pharaoh called Thutmosis III, whose character and death fits perfectly with the biblical story of the last great pharaoh of the oppression. In fact, as we looked into the life of Pharaoh Amenhotep II, he met condition after condition, until there was only one more to complete! The Bible specifically mentions that the first-born son of the exodus pharaoh dies in the judgments of God, Exodus 12:29. If Amenhotep II is the exodus pharaoh, then his first-born son must have died and cannot succeed him as pharaoh. We knew we would have to enter the tomb of the successor to Amenhotep II to discover if he was the first-born son. His successor was Thutmosis IV and if he was the first-born son of Amenhotep, then this man could not be the exodus pharaoh!

In the valley we entered many of the tombs of the pharaohs seeking clues in our search. Whilst our most anticipated tomb was that of Thutmosis IV. Inside his sarcophagus sits quietly, visited by few.

Our research into the life and times of Pharaoh Amenhotep II and Pharaoh Thutmosis IV took a considerable amount of time, and visiting these tombs was for us the final fulfilment to many years of inquiry into the question of the exodus evidence.

The answer to the question of the successor to Amenhotep II was finally settled at the pyramids. Just in front of the Great Sphinx of Giza, resides a large tablet called the Dream Stela of Thutmosis IV. In this large record of ancient times, Pharaoh Thutmosis IV argues that he is the rightful successor of Amenhotep II, though clearly he was not the first-born son! In the Dream Stela Thutmosis IV claims whilst dreaming, the Sphinx which was buried in the sand appeared to him and said, "Uncover me and you shall become king of Egypt." This record shows an attempt by Thutmosis IV to justify that he was the rightful heir, even though he was not the first-born. This proves that Amenhotep II's first-born son never succeeded him, making him an ideal candidate for the exodus pharaoh.

Our mission in the Valley of the Kings was complete and we ran down the valley as we departed. Later as we compared the ten conditions found in the Bible for the exodus pharaoh, we confirmed Amenhotep II met every one! He is the only one to come to power at the exact time the Bible predicts, with a vile oppressive predecessor, and the death of his first-born son fits in precisely with the Bible. Scholars remain sceptical about all. However if the clues from the Bible, including its timeline are followed, the facts about his life make Amenhotep II the primary candidate for the exodus pharaoh.

We entered many tombs in the Valley of the Kings. This belonged to Thutmosis III. The excavations here made our visit unforgettable.

Seeing the Face of the Exodus Pharaoh
'Moses was eighty years old...when they spoke to pharaoh' Exodus 7:7.

The first reference to ancient Israel outside of the Bible is found in Egypt after the time of Pharaoh Ramesses II. This fact joined with the references to the city of Ramesses in the Bible, are two of the key factors why scholars often identify Ramesses II as the forgotten exodus pharaoh. However, to do this one has to reject a strict interpretation of the Bible timeline. In addition, the existence of Israel as described in the Bible until its demise would need to be dramatically shortened to acquiesce with the Ramesses II timeline. We believe that the Bible's description of its own history is accurate; therefore we cannot compromise the biblical record of history to fit in with the ever challenged opinion of Egyptian chronology. Our research and that of strict biblical scholars states that the exodus took place around 1446 B.C. In our search for the exodus pharaoh, we believe only one man truly meets all the requirements as the Bible suggests to fulfil such a role. That man is Pharaoh Amenhotep II. He lived at the right time, came to power during the age when the Bible states Moses returns to confront a new pharaoh, and his first-born son does not succeed him. In addition, we find it compelling that Pharaoh Amenhotep II is relatively unknown - forgotten in history. It strikes us that the Bible itself shows a great deal of contempt for the exodus pharaoh, because he's not even worth mentioning by name. This would not be the case for Ramesses II, who was one of the greatest pharaohs in ancient Egyptian history. However there are a copious number of reasons to consider Amenhotep II to be the exodus pharaoh, including being preceded by a vicious pharaoh. Pharaoh Thutmosis III, the great oppressor carried out seventeen military campaigns, but his son Amenhotep II, only carried out three. What happened to turn an aggressive Egypt into a shy and reluctant state? According to the biblical timeline, the Hebrew slaves left Egypt in 1446 B.C., this would have left Egypt short of slave labour. Yet Egyptian history tells us that Amenhotep II was only able to carry out one more war after 1446 B.C., and this war was against a people group who were weak and insignificant.

In the Egyptian records, Amenhotep II states he took over 100,000 slaves captive in his last war. Could this final war have been undertaken for the purpose of replacing the Hebrew slaves?

Pharaoh Amenhotep II has met all the biblical conditions to be considered as the exodus pharaoh and he has left posterity with a plethora of impressions of himself. By analysing these images of Pharaoh Amenhotep II to pinpoint key characteristics, and by comparing them with details of physical anthropology, cultural and archaeological data, we can use modern technology to recreate an artist's impression of Pharaoh Amenhotep II.

Now for the first time in over three millennia, we can look at the face of the most likely candidate for the exodus pharaoh!

Scholars will argue forever over the identity of the exodus pharaoh. However, until a verified artefact is found which settles the matter by clearly identifying this pharaoh, we believe Amenhotep II has a case which remains biblically formidable. "Indeed for this purpose I have raised you up, that I may show My power in you and that My name may be declared in all the earth" Exodus 9:16. This verse indicates the Lord raised the exodus pharaoh up, so God would be glorified worldwide for delivering Israel from Egypt.

The Bible Plagues and Egyptian History
"I will harden pharaoh's heart and multiply My signs and My wonders in the land of Egypt" Exodus 7:3.

The Bible tells us that Moses confronted pharaoh and told him to let God's people go. Pharaoh refused, therefore God sent a series of devastating judgments on the land of Egypt, and some believe that an ancient Egyptian papyrus records these acts of God. The Ipuwer Papyrus now resides in the National Archaeological Museum in Leiden, the Netherlands and its contents are unparalleled.

In the exodus account the Bible says, 'All the waters that were in the river turned to blood' Exodus 7:20. The papyrus says, 'The river was turned to blood.' The Bible says, 'The Lord sent thunder and hail and fire darted to the ground...so there was hail and fire' Exodus 9:23-24. The papyrus says, 'Fire ran along the ground. There was hail and fire.' The Bible says, 'Locusts went up over all the land of Egypt and they ate' everything Exodus 10:14-15. The papyrus says, 'Grain has perished on every side...no fruit or herbs are found.' The Bible says, 'There was thick darkness in the land of Egypt' Exodus 10:22. The papyrus says, 'The land is not light.' The Bible says, 'The Lord struck all the first-born in the land of Egypt' Exodus 12:29. The papyrus says, 'He who places his brother in the ground is everywhere.' The Bible says, 'There was a great cry in Egypt' Exodus 12:30. The papyrus says, 'Groaning is throughout the land, mingled with lamentations.'

When this papyrus was first interpreted, it was believed by many to be the Egyptian account of the biblical plagues. However many scholars today suggest it may describe the fall of the Old Kingdom. Nevertheless, for some biblical scholars the unprecedented association with the Bible's account seems to indicate this document describes the same events as chronicled in Scripture. Therefore with limited information available, the dating could feasibly be inaccurate. At the very least, this papyrus confirms the disasters that overtook Egypt in the Bible are not only plausible, but documented.

One of the most interesting records of the Ipuwer Papyrus is the account of the River Nile turning to blood, as mentioned in the Bible.

According to the Bible, after a series of judgments from God, Moses led the Hebrew slaves out of Egypt, and ancient Israel witnessed one of the greatest miracles of history - the parting of the Red Sea. Yet the location of the Red Sea is still a mystery. What was the Red Sea? Where is it today and where did the Hebrews cross? We pursued the answers to these questions.

The parting of the Red Sea is central to the exodus story, but no-one has proved conclusively where their crossing took place. We know the starting point for the exodus was the area of Ramesses (Avaris), and one traditional idea is the Hebrews headed south and crossed the tip of the Red Sea. However, in the Hebrew text the body of water the Hebrews crossed is literally called, "Yam-Suph." This was translated as the Red Sea, yet many believe its true meaning is, "Sea of Reeds." The Sea of Reeds would refer to a lake where reeds were abundant; some of these lakes can still be found - they are deep enough to drown in, and are shallow enough to be parted by a strong east wind.

The Sea of Reeds interpretation of the Hebrew Bible opens up new possibilities and it also presents us with major problems. We can find lakes in the Nile Delta now, but the building of the Suez Canal reconfigured this area and dried up old lakes. Trying to find what this area would have looked liked three thousand five hundred years ago is unfortunately almost impossible. However, in recent years NASA has released some of its early satellite images of Egypt and they are very helpful in this search. By studying NASA satellite photos of Egypt before recent development and data from specialist image equipment, experts were able to find the imprint of the missing lakes in the Nile Delta, to help us visualise the region during the time of Moses. This data gives us four possible options for the crossing - the Northern Lake, El-Ballah Lake, Lake Timsah or the Bitter Lake.

The NASA satellite photos also helped reveal the outline of several old forts on the Northern Route, which the Bible calls The Way of the Philistines. According to Scripture, God told Moses not to take this Northern Route, "Lest perhaps the people change their minds when they see war" Exodus 13:17. The Northern Route which the Bible identifies has been found and was called The Way of Horus by the Egyptians. As the Northern Route was forbidden it seems unlikely that the Hebrews would have crossed at the Northern Lake. This leaves us with three more options for the crossing - the El-Ballah Lake, Lake Timsah or the Bitter Lake.

One of the modern favourite locations for the Red Sea crossing is the Gulf of Aqaba (p.66). During the time of Solomon, the Gulf of Aqaba was called the Red Sea, yet references in the Bible to the Gulf of Aqaba using this title are few. However, if this is the Red Sea that the Hebrews crossed, then there are two possible locations for the crossing - one in the south, where the shallow waters have allowed a coral reef to grow and in the north, where an underwater ridge has been discovered.

When we arrived at the Gulf of Aqaba bordering Saudi Arabia, our research had cast doubts over this concept. The primary reason for this concern is the importance of the position of the Red Sea in location to the site of Mount Sinai. If the Hebrews crossed the Gulf of Aqaba, then logic dictates that the mountain of God must be in Saudi Arabia. When we first began our inquiry we had no preconceived ideas to the precise location of Mount Sinai. If it was in the Sinai Peninsula or in Saudi Arabia, it really didn't matter to us. But as we carried out our research over a matter of years, it became obvious that the body of opinion lies with Mount Sinai residing in the Sinai Peninsula, and this means the Gulf of Aqaba crossing is improbable. Having said all of that, the only opinion that could forever transform our search for the Red Sea was the biblical text itself, and the more we looked at the Bible, the more it seemed to confirm that Mount Sinai is located somewhere in the Sinai Peninsula. This conclusion makes the Gulf of Aqaba theory null and void. We'll explain why in our search for Mount Sinai.

We always knew that our examination of the exodus case would involve deliberating over all the theories and weighing all the objections to these theories. In this light, we believe we can find the most credible of the scenarios. Therefore, at this point we have to accept that trying to find 'the exact' point of the crossing, without any reliable inscriptions is impossible. Many have tried to use the details the Bible gives to identify locations where the Hebrews travelled; but none have been able to present a credible scenario that can be tested, tried and be accepted by the body of opinion. As the Bible says, 'The first to present his case seems right, until another comes forward and questions him' Proverbs 18:17.

It would be wonderful to be able to claim to have finally settled the location of the Red Sea, yet the reality is that no one has been able to do this. There are many theories and many have claimed to have created a cast-iron case for one location or another; but those who have

studied all the subject matter have found there is a lot more to consider than just a few nice images and theories. For Christians, we believe by faith that the people of Israel did indeed cross through "Yam-Suph." Nevertheless, where the crossing took place is still a mystery. Visitors to Egypt may well be sailing a boat over it, or it may have been one of the dried up lakes we drove over!

In recent years, almost all the attention for the search for Mount Sinai has been placed in Saudi Arabia. Nevertheless, for almost two thousand years Christians have located this mountain in the Sinai Peninsula, in modern-day Egypt - could they all be wrong? Is it really possible that Mount Sinai could be in Saudi Arabia?

For decades now, claims have been made for Saudi Arabia to be the location for Mount Sinai. However, devout biblical scholars have often questioned the Saudi Arabian theories, and of all the items and photographs that have been proposed as final evidence for these claims, none have been independently tested or verified.

When we began to scrutinise these claims, we had no preference to the location of Mount Sinai. If it turned up in Egypt or in Saudi Arabia, it made no difference to us. Yet as we kept reading the Scriptures and the best research of Bible-believing scholars, we found the biblical text itself is compelling in its objections to the claims of Saudi Arabia as the location for the mountain of God. The Bible's chronicle of the exodus story itself seems to indicate that Mount Sinai is located in the Sinai Peninsula.

The primary reason for the misunderstanding about the location of this mountain is the misinterpretation of Saint Paul's statement in Galatians 4:25. When the Apostle Paul wrote of Arabia as the location for Mount Sinai, he was not using a twenty-first century map as his geographical reference point! The Apostle Paul was a child of the Roman age, holding Roman citizenship and he often used Roman names to record locations. For the Romans at the time of Paul, the Sinai Peninsula was part of Arabia and when Rome later wrestled control of the Sinai Peninsula from the Nabataeans in the second century, they named their new province according to their two traditional names - Arabia Petraea. Therefore, when Paul wrote that the mountain which Moses ascended was in Arabia, he was not identifying the first Saudi state (1744-1818), the second Saudi state (1824-1891) or the present day state of Saudi Arabia, founded in 1900 - he was writing of the Roman world's Arabia. To conclude, Paul was not correcting the author of the book of Exodus, relocating Mount Sinai to another region, but rather re-confirming that Mount Sinai is in Arabia, which included the Sinai Peninsula.

Sometimes people claim that Mount Sinai must be in Saudi Arabia, because it is 'out of Egypt,' just like the journey of ancient Israel. Yet, students of ancient Egyptian history know that the Egyptian hold on the Sinai Peninsula changed over time. There is a great difference between making a technical claim to an area and literally occupying it. In the time of Moses, vast areas of the Sinai Peninsula were out of Egypt's literal control. Another example of the misinterpretation of the biblical text concerns the story of Midian in the Bible. The land of Midian has been identified as the north-western part of modern-day Saudi Arabia and Moses' life in this area has led to confusion about the location of Mount Sinai. The story of Moses at the burning bush can also be misinterpreted to suggest the Midian location for Mount Sinai. However, an exegesis of the text and an understanding of the culture indicates that Moses led his flocks from Midian, not into it, Exodus 3. We must remember that Bedouin shepherds often travelled very long distances with their flocks and Moses most probably often left Midian with the flocks.

When one quickly reads the passages concerning Moses in Midian, it's very easy for the mind to read Midian, Midian, Midian and then Mount Sinai. This first impression makes it appear that the mountain is located in Midian. Yet students of hermeneutics who study these passages make it clear that this is an error which comes from reading the passages too speedily without a forensic approach. Exodus chapter 18 leaves no doubt that the mountain of God is not in modern-day Saudi Arabia/Midian. Moses' father-in-law leaves his home in Midian (Saudi Arabia) and meets Moses at Mount Sinai, Exodus 18:1-6,27. Later, 'Moses let his father-in-law depart (from Mount Sinai) and he went his way to his own land' (Saudi Arabia). In Numbers 10:29-33, Moses' father-in-law confirms again that Mount Sinai is not in Midian, by stating on this second occasion at the mountain, "I will depart to my own land." The text is clear.

The Exodus Route
'They moved from the Red Sea and camped
in the wilderness of sin' Numbers 33:11.

As we prepared for our expedition into the Sinai Peninsula, we remembered the warnings of troubles we had received. Before our journey we were informed that everything in the Middle East has political fallout. Many years ago Egypt made peace with modern Israel and immediately it faced the wrath of her neighbours. For some, this marked a turning point where Egypt lost some of its standing in the Muslim world. Since that time Egypt has worked hard to restore its position of leadership in the Middle East, and we were warned that no-one wanted to promote any evidence that has been found which may support Israel's historic presence in the land. With that fresh in our minds, we also had concern for the general stability of the region during these troubled times.

As we drove into the Sinai Peninsula, we found the area in virtual lockdown. There were checkpoints all over and we knew exactly why. Just a few days before the police had stopped a car loaded with explosives, and afterwards one of Egypt's borders was blown up, which led to tens of thousands of foreigners storming into Egypt. The government was trying hard to gain control without losing face. In the midst of this drama, we kept a low profile with a hope we could fulfil our mission without any interference.

As we entered the Sinai Peninsula, our first thoughts went towards the ancient Hebrew slaves who would have walked on one of the routes we were taking. It was somewhere in this area that ancient Israel took its long walk to freedom. As we pondered this, we re-examined our research to question what route they would have taken. Our hunt for the Red Sea left us with three plausible candidates for the Red Sea miracle. Therefore if this is the case, then three routes into the wilderness are plausible - the Way of Shur, the Arabian Trade Route and finally the Traditional Route.

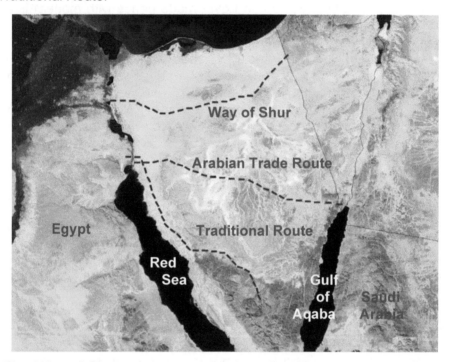

The Way of Shur passes near Kadesh Barnea, which according to Deuteronomy 1:2, was eleven days journey from Mount Sinai; but was this route too dangerously close to the forbidden Northern Route? Did they really reach Mount Sinai along this route so quickly? The book of Exodus says, 'In the third month after the children of Israel had gone out of the land of Egypt...they came to the wilderness of Sinai and...Israel camped there before the mountain' Exodus 19:1-2. This route therefore seems too direct for the Scriptural clues. The Bible explains Moses fled from Egypt aged forty and lived in Midian for forty years. Midian has been clearly identified to be in modern-day Saudi Arabia. So it is interesting that the Arabian Trade Route would have been the direct route for Moses to flee from Egypt into Midian. So was this the route the Hebrews later took? Finally there is the Traditional Route. It's not very direct, but the Bible does reveal the Israelites wandered around in the wilderness for a very long time, and the hostile environment fits in well with the terrain. In addition Jeremiah 2:6 indicates that ancient Israel did not travel on a trading route saying, "Where is the Lord that brought us up out of the land of Egypt, who led us through the wilderness, through a land of deserts and pits, through a land of drought and of the shadow of death, through a land that no man crossed and where no man dwelt?"

Critics state because of the harsh terrain, it would have been impossible for Israel to travel through much of the Sinai Peninsula. Nevertheless, the Bible makes it exceptionally clear that the journey was one of terrible hardships. It took no time at all for the Hebrews to complain and they ended up weeping because of thirst, and cried out, "Why is it you have brought us up out of Egypt to kill us and our children and our livestock with thirst?" Exodus 17:3.

In the Sinai Peninsula, we found large areas suitable for making camp and we could understand the logistical troubles of travelling through small routes, with high valleys on both sides. After all our research and travels in this region, for us the biblical text seems to indicate the possibility of two major options for the exodus route - the Traditional Route with Mount Sinai in the south, or a central route with Mount Sinai somewhere along the way.

Once again it would be nice to be able to claim to have 'solved the mystery' and to produce a map with a completed itinerary for ancient Israel. Yet this is not presently possible. We know from Egyptian records that many of the place names the Hebrews visited were recognisable locations, but three thousand five hundred years later, the terrain has changed too much. History has wiped away all traces of ancient Israel. The conundrum of their route is still an enigma.

We believe by faith that the Hebrews fled through this area of the world and it is faith that sustains our confidence. As for the exact route, well, no doubt many will continue to publish interesting maps and other materials claiming to have resolutely settled the question. However, without an ancient inscription or the discovery of an authentic artefact that can help in the search, we all continue to play with proposed paths and new itineraries. Debates persist, questions are raised, advocates issue theories and critics continue to embrace incredulity. This is the nature of research and archaeology. It is the constant questioning which helps to keep any veritable search credible. Claiming to have solved the mystery of the exodus route is one thing, proving it categorically is another.

Mount Horeb is one of the two names the Hebrew Bible gives to the holy mountain which acquired renowned status through the promulgation of the Law. In rabbinical literature, the rabbis propose Sinai and Horeb are the two names for the same mountain, and the New Testament writers confirm they are both one and the same, by obviating Horeb in favour of Sinai.

We have already discovered that trying to take Mount Sinai out of the Sinai Peninsula is biblically unfounded. In addition, it can be unwise to rely too much on other ancient literature in the search for this mountain, for it is possible to use the works of the historian Josephus to support the case for many locations. However, his key statement is that Mount Sinai was 'the highest peak,' which in the Sinai Peninsula at 2629 metres is Mount Catherine. Yet, historians inform us that we must be careful when dealing with the works of Josephus, because he was prone to a little exaggeration.

Our search for Mount Sinai began by scrutinising suggested sites for the mountain. We found about ten proposed sites, suggested by scholars, amateur adventurers and prominent TV producers. We always knew the search for this peak would be united with the search for the exodus route; and as the central and traditional routes through the Peninsula had risen to prominence, we summarised that the mountain

of God must be near to one of these routes. Yet, we always found ourselves asking one question, "What would one need to find to prove the location of Mount Sinai?"

The question of security in this region was constantly reinforced by the guards stationed everywhere. Still amongst all the suggested sites in the Peninsula there is only one that has claimed authenticity for over a millennium. Our mission was to enter St. Katherine's monastery, which is located at the base of the traditional site of Mount Sinai and to test its claims of authenticity. After a drive we entered one of the oldest Christian sites in the world. We witnessed ancient Christian art and found the original home of some of the earliest biblical manuscripts. The ancient origins of this site are indisputable and to casually dismiss it would be a sign of the tragedy of the modern age. Yet at the same time, we found nothing which could finally settle their claim to be the location of Mount Sinai.

We wish we could declare, "We've found Mount Sinai!" However, this has happened many times before, yet the exploration still continues. Constantly we found ourselves going back to our original question and asking, "What would one need to find to prove the location of Mount Sinai?" As we pondered this question, we deduced that perhaps Scripture does give us an answer. There is only one way to finally settle the question of the location of Mount Sinai, and this is to find an ancient inscription which can be tested and tried in the light of all. But does such an inscription exist?

The Bible states Moses spoke with God on Mount Sinai and 'He gave Moses two tablets of the Testimony, tablets of stone, written with the finger of God. Then Moses turned and went down from the mountain and the two tablets of the Testimony were in his hands.' When he saw Israel worshipping an idol his 'anger became hot and he cast the tablets out of his hands and broke them at the foot of the mountain' Exodus 32. Moses later received two new tablets; whilst the fate of the first tablets, written with the finger of God is still unknown. Could it be that somewhere in this region, buried deep beneath the sand at the base of a mountain, Moses' two broken tablets of the Testimony remain lost, just waiting to be found?

We spent the morning at Saint Katherine's monastery viewing priceless art, comparing ancient biblical manuscripts and looking for inspiration for our ascent of the traditional site of Mount Sinai. One of the modern items to view was the signature of Napoleon who promised to protect this monastery on his campaign in Egypt.

The mountain of Jebel Musa itself is 2285 metres high and for local Bedouins and Christians, it is the location of Mount Sinai. We found no cogent evidence here to confirm this theory. Nonetheless, we always need to approach the claims of this region, which were made over a millennium ago with humility; instead of the contempt which is often shown. There is a danger in this age that we treat with condescension the most important decision these pilgrims ever made, which shaped their entire lives over fifteen centuries ago. Some foolishly believe the monastical commitment of the first pilgrims here, began with a foolhardy game of Russian Roulette, as if they pointed out any peak and said, "That will do." If you were going to spend your life as a monk at Mount Sinai, would you make such a commitment without a deep sense of certainty of its authenticity? Nevertheless, such a belief is not proof.

Expectation began to grow as we touched the base of this mountain. For more than a millennium pilgrims have come here to seek the mountain upon which Moses met with God. Somewhere in this region Moses received the Ten Commandments. Could it have been here?

Research has demonstrated that this mountain may not be the mountain which Moses visited, but there is no absolute proof that it is not. We came here with the hope of experiencing an ascent of a mountain, just like the one Moses would have climbed. This was a small part of the journey where our search was not for fact, but for feeling. We knew there was no inscription to see, just an experience to have. We had planned a five hour ascent, giving us time to stop, photograph and film along the way. Our hope was to catch the sunset, but on the way up the weather conditions began to change and other visitors began to abandon the summit attempt.

When we prepared for this expedition up the traditional site of Mount Sinai, we had no idea how extraordinary the experience would be. A few hours into the hike, we found a fluttering of snow falling on the ground and settling. As we moved up higher and higher, the snow began to get thicker. One hour away from the completion of our ascent, we began to understand why so many people visiting had abandoned the summit. On some of the higher paths, the snow having been walked on began to turn to ice. A stony path covered with ice was a dangerous combination and the risk of slipping was great. But for us, we knew that our summit must be now or never, and so with great caution, we were the last that day willing to take the calculated risk to get to the top.

On our final push to the top, we broke through the snow and the summit came into sight. When we began this hike we believed our time here would be another casual ascent, but the snow and the fact we were the last people at the top made it a very special moment indeed. We had come here seeking an experience and as we walked on ice-covered stone to reach the top, we felt isolated, exhausted and motivated. Moses may or may not have come here, but for us the memories of this ascent will last forever.

The Pharaoh who Fought Ancient Israel
'In those days there was no king in Israel;
everyone did what was right in his
own eyes' Judges 21:25.

It is a breathtaking adventure to enter an ancient tomb or a temple. However, if you haven't completed any research beforehand, you won't know what you are looking at. Around Egypt we found many tourists stood mystified before guides as they read off one pharaoh's name after another. The look on their faces showed they had become submerged in data and all was lost in an overloaded gaze of uncertainty. This is one of the reasons why we spent years studying ancient Egypt before we embarked upon this quest. It's not enough to see a tomb or enter one, we must first understand it.

During our years of research the name of one pharaoh kept coming up time and time again. We knew this man would become a prominent figure in our expedition, but who was he? His name was Pharaoh Merneptah. This man was the thirteenth son of Ramesses II and he was in his sixties or older when he came to power. Pharaoh Merneptah commenced the demise of the sweeping and elegant city of Pi-Ramesses by moving the administrative capital of Egypt back to ancient Memphis. Yet it was his wars which made him famous and one particular war with a people group called Israel!

In modern-day Luxor, we spoke to the locals to get directions to find the temple of Pharaoh Merneptah. After probing for answers we were given the keys to discover what we were looking for. We were told to cross the River Nile, pass by the colossal statues and walk through the

buried temple into the fallen Temple of Merneptah. Inside the biblical people of Israel are mentioned!

Following the clues we received, we passed by the colossal statues and walked through the buried temple. Then we entered Pharaoh Merneptah's fallen temple. The broken remains of this overlooked temple keep a great secret; hidden away from the sun in a special area, the treasures of this temple reside.

From the outside this temple looks like a disarrayed combination of toppled stones. For this reason few visitors know of, or take the time to find the stolen treasures used to build Merneptah's temple.

The undervalued images inside this temple are overwhelming. They include some astonishingly well preserved polychrome reliefs of Amenhotep III, which are some of the finest examples in Egypt. However, it is outside where the most precious artefact is found.

There is nothing uncomplicated in the search for the exodus. Every artefact has a story, every story has a setting, every setting has an interpretation, and every interpretation is preceded by a worldview. Then we must recall that every worldview is clouded by prejudice, every prejudice is guided by culture, and every culture is forged by a comprehensive set of unobserved attitudes, beliefs, behaviours and characteristics. In the Western world many currently have an undertide of contempt for the accuracy of the biblical account, and this often finds its way into the work of scholars, who are often afraid to confront their own scepticism and the reasons behind it.

In the modern age we comfort ourselves with the myth of unbiased news, analysis and history. Anyone claiming complete impartiality reveals how truly biased he or she is. In the context of archaeology and the interpretation of artefacts, we are all in danger of subjecting a predetermined belief or opinion into the act of interpretation. When we began our investigation we realised we needed not only to understand the varying interpretations of the artefacts found, but the story behind the interpretations. It became obvious whilst studying the works of great scholars that some were hostile towards the Bible, and their proposals were grounded, even stranded in their personal doubt. Whilst other successful scholars had an open mind and their interpretations of the same objects reflect their beliefs too. This is one of the reasons why two scholars studying the same artefact can come to entirely different conclusions to its meaning.

Our search for the exodus evidence is of course, a reflection upon our belief that the exodus did indeed take place. Our stated purpose clarifies our position; yet often we had to read between the lines when studying the labour of others. We have even found that some scholars have chosen to virtually ignore significant evidence in their presentations - most importantly the record of Pharaoh Merneptah.

The Bible states that after entering the land of Canaan, the people of Israel soon fell into anarchy. Without a clear succession of leadership, the assertion became 'every man for himself.' The Bible records these events in the book of Judges and with a strict interpretation of the biblical timeline, Israel would be in this state of anarchy during the time of Pharaoh Merneptah and others. Scholars who reject the biblical timeline often place the exodus hundreds of years later than the Bible, yet for us the Bible is our guide.

We had been hoping to find the evidence that Egypt recognised the existence of the ancient people of Israel living in the land of Canaan. Then, in front of us was the very thing we had been looking for. The Merneptah stela contains irrefutable evidence that 3,200 years ago, the people of Israel were living in Canaan as a distinct people group.

The stela of Pharaoh Merneptah contains the first reference to ancient Israel outside of the Bible! The text records Merneptah's talk of victories against his enemies. Excerpts from it state: 'Canaan is captive with all woe. Ashkelon is conquered...Israel is laid waste, its seed is no more.' The name

Israel is followed by a throw-stick denoting a foreigner and then by a sign-group of a seated man and woman. Below them are three plural strokes. This confirms that Israel was a people group, not a nation - just as the Bible's book of Judges suggests. Israel can be found in hieroglyphics!

In the hunt for a correlation between ancient Israel and Egypt, there are few objects which can be claimed to be 'irrefutable evidence,' yet the stela of Pharaoh Merneptah is one herculean exception to this rule. This record proves beyond all contradiction that a people group called Israel lived in Canaan around 1200 B.C. Not too along ago sceptical scholars stated it was inconceivable that such a people existed in this age. Now this record demonstrates that ancient Israel lived, not in the fairyland of myth, but they co-existed in an age with the great pharaohs of ancient Egypt!

This record indicates that Israel was well established in Canaan by 1200 B.C. and it also demonstrates the unreliability of Egyptian records. Pharaoh Merneptah boasts he committed genocide against Israel, by wiping them off the face of the earth. This is an obvious case of propaganda and makes us wonder what other records in Egypt have been falsified. The stela dates to the time of the Judges in the Bible, and the word 'Israel' is written with the determinative for 'a people' rather than 'a nation.' The Bible tells us that the time of Judges was an age of chaos, as central leadership broke down, therefore the Bible and the stela agree. This stela is in fact a copy of the original in the Egyptian Museum, which we also visited.

Scholars doubt the story of Israel's conquest of Canaan, yet this stela helps confirm it. It affirms Israel's existence in the land and in Judges 1:29, we learn Israel could not defeat the city of Gezer. But Merneptah, with his army took the city that the Bible says Israel left independent. The stela says, 'Gezer has been captured.'

The Merneptah chronicle also teaches us about the 'Russian Roulette' element of archaeology. The Merneptah stela proves that there was an ancient people called Israel living in their land by 1200 B.C. Yet if this stone was still buried in Egypt, the next mention of Israel outside of the Bible is found four hundred years later! If the Merneptah stela was still buried, archaeologists would be telling us that ancient Israel only existed by the time of 800 B.C., based on the Moabite stone and later Assyrian records. However, the Merneptah stela gives us a permanent date for the existence of ancient Israel that cannot be dismissed - the Bible was right after all and perhaps there are other artefacts still buried in Egypt which will reveal more. Pharaoh Merneptah claimed that he destroyed the people of Israel, but actually this pharaoh left us with the evidence which decimated the weak theories of sceptical scholars, who once claimed that no such people ever existed during this age.

Archaeology and the Exodus
'But these things are written that you
may believe...' John 20:31.

Our investigation into the exodus case is now complete and as we stopped to look back upon our quest, we felt astonished at all the discoveries we had seen. We had witnessed scenes of Semitic people entering Egypt wearing multi-coloured coats like Joseph. We found Semitic settlements in the Bible's land of Goshen and perhaps we even saw the face of Joseph. All over ancient Egypt we found bricks made with straw and our eyes beheld Semitic slaves making bricks just as the Bible describes. On our adventures here, we had visited lost cities, and entered the tombs and temples of the pharaohs in our quest to find Moses. We hunted for the Red Sea, traced the exodus routes and perhaps we even came close to seeing the exodus pharaoh face to face. Finally we have examined the first reference to ancient Israel outside of the Bible.

When we began our search for the exodus many years ago, we knew we would need to scrutinize an outstanding number of great works. Yet, as authors and broadcasters we realised that what we learnt would be published in books, posted on the internet and broadcast on TV channels around the world. We knew our mission was not to prepare another theory, but to test and probe all the ideas that scholars and sceptics have presented over the years, to examine each theory and then to prepare a broad presentation.

There are genuine complications in the search for the Bible's exodus. Yet historians and archaeologists have always battled with the inconsistencies and contentions of the past. In England, we are not even sure if some of our ancient kings were real. Therefore, imagine the dilemma of trying to locate illiterate and inconsequential slaves who lived on the Nile's floodplain thirty-five centuries ago!

Critics may suggest that far too much of the exodus related material is circumstantial. However we could ask - who in the ancient world paid their best artists to create stone monuments dedicated to the service of slaves? What nation dedicated a temple to a military defeat inflicted by fleeing captives, and who records the worst economic disaster of a generation in a bombastic memorial?

In every nation and generation, we find people trying to falsify claims to greatness, but forging claims to slavery? Who does that?

Every great nation cherishes a partisan view of their story. America is the land of the free, Britain is the mother of the free and China is the Middle Kingdom, representing five thousand years of astounding history. Yet ancient Israel recorded their story by claiming to be the descendants of a subjugated people, whose capital qualities were grumbling and idolatry. Their great escape out of Egypt began with altercations, repulsion at the interference of Moses and immediate disparagement of God's intervention. Just after the greatest miracle of their history, the mood was soon one of hostility, antagonism, acrimony, repulsion, revenge and loathing. They quickly ran out of water, lacked new provisions and Moses was confronted with the animosity of his people, which led to civil war. The Israelites even began to plan their return to slavery in Egypt. These accounts do not feel like the propaganda of a people trying to falsify their history, but the story of the human condition. We can all identify with their doubts, complaining, challenges and aspirations.

Even if an ancient and direct reference to the exodus is one day found in Egypt, shifting the burden of proof, scholars will continue to debate. Yet the chronicle of the exodus will forever remain as one of the most powerful, influential and lasting stories of human history. People can doubt it, others can choose by faith to believe it. But what we cannot do is stop it! Over three thousand years later, the exodus account is still alive and well - this year the exodus story will be heard by millions in Africa, Asia, Europe and in the Americas. It is a cultural force that has swept through world history and its narrative will forever illuminate, challenge and inspire every generation. It is their story and it is our story.

With the hunt for the exodus evidence behind us, our quest led us to search for the other great treasures of the Bible. What happened to the gold and silver of King David and his successors, and where is ancient Israel's greatest treasure - the lost Ark of the Covenant?

According to the Bible, the design of the Ark of the Covenant was given to Moses on Mount Sinai by God. When my brother and I walked down the traditional site of the mountain in the dark, Mathew suddenly turned to me and said, "Paul, look up!" During the descent our eyes had been pinned to the ground, making sure we did not lose our footing and fall in the dark, and therefore we had missed the heavens above. As I looked up to the sky, I was amazed. Never before had I seen such a sight. Due to light pollution, the stars which I had seen from Britain seemed small, delicate and distant. However, in this desert I saw many thousands of gleaming balls of light overwhelming the sky. The darkness was squeezed out of the sky, with numerous stars three times the size I had ever seen before, circled by thousands of smaller glows of light. For the first time, I began to understand the challenge and promise to Abraham, "Count the stars, if you are able to number them...so shall your descendants be." As I gazed upward, I knew I could not count them. They were in my mind without number - an extravagant witness of the shining and shimmering promise to the Father of the Jews. Hundreds of years later, the Bible confirms that this promise was being fulfilled as a substantial force of Hebrew slaves escaped out of Egypt, to converge at Mount Sinai. It was during this solemn assembly that Moses had a vision from God to build the Ark of the Covenant. The Ark became the most sacred object to the ancient people of Israel and was placed inside Solomon's Temple (artist's impression below). After Solomon's death the Kingdom was divided into Israel and Judah; this demarcation weakened the people of the Bible, and made them easy pickings for the predatory nations and empires that invaded Jerusalem, and stole their wealth. It was in this context that the Ark of the Covenant was lost to history.

The Ark of the Covenant bequeaths us with many of the greatest unanswered questions of the Bible. What did the Ark look like? Where did it go? When did it disappear and does it still exist?

The Bible's Ark has captured the imagination like no other sacred object of antiquity, and over many centuries adventurers have searched and presented theories concerning the lost Ark. Many of these conclusions teach us more about the power of the human imagination, rather than the history of the Ark itself. Archaeologists and explorers have spent millions chasing shadows, rumours and interpretations of ancient texts in their search for the Ark, and they all are transfixed by one tantalising question - How could something so distinguished and powerful vanish from history?

In this investigation into the mystery of the lost Ark of the Covenant we have discovered that some have projected their own desires and creative dreams into their hunt for answers, seeing things that no-one else has seen and claiming to have found secret chambers, lost routes and artefacts that never materialise. The 'evidence' is always just around the next corner, yet always out of sight. Many have followed legends, maps and speculative fantasies with the hope of solving the oldest question about the world's most famous treasure.

With these warnings in mind, we wanted to be assured that our quest would not be one into our own imagination, but founded on the cornerstone of rigorous analysis, trusted scholarship, logical research and verifiable artefacts. Ruling out theories, refuting legends and using research to eliminate claims has been just as important in this pursuit, as probing for empirical data.

As we begin this inquiry into the enigma of the Ark, we must first concede that we never expected to partake in a mission to 'hunt for the Ark of the Covenant.' This was never a secret hope, a private plan or dream, yet through a series of unexpected events, we found ourselves in the right place, at the right time and with access to a great deal of research on the subject. We also knew we would not partake in the work of excavation, but rather of exploration.

In this task, we intend to carry out a veracious autopsy of the many claims to have located the Ark; to do this we need to vigorously check and challenge every cognitive intent, idea, sentiment, theory, and alleged find. Before us was a remarkable journey which would lead to ancient Egyptian tombs, desert cities, lost civilisations and to a cornucopia of claims and legends that need thorough assessing.

The Bible, Faith and Archaeology
'That we should no longer be children, tossed to and fro and carried about with every wind of doctrine' Ephesians 4:14.

There are over two billion Christians, who according to orthodox teaching believe that the Bible is God's revelation to man. These believers represent the largest majority of any religious group or worldview on earth. No other faith has played such an enormous role in shaping the world as Christianity has and for this reason the Bible is the most vigorously contested book in world history.

The debate into the history of the Bible's text has split experts and archaeologists into three camps; those who trust in the reliability of Scripture, those who believe there is an element of truth and those who are convinced that most, if not all is fiction. The great multitudes of people therefore find themselves like a sail boat in the ocean, blown about by every wind and wave of opinion. For this reason, people receive contradictory messages concerning the stories of the Bible and archaeological evidence. For example, if an individual watches an expert on TV suggesting that a certain event in the Bible never took place, doubt is formed. But then, the same person goes on to read another study by an expert which comes to the opposite conclusion. Confusion is the outcome - who is telling the truth? Within this context, there appears to be two ways of approaching the Bible and archaeology. The first is to present an opinion about the veracity of the biblical text based on what has not been found; the second is to present an opinion based on what has been found. The secular media tend to take the first approach, whilst many Christians are oblivious to the biblical finds which have been made.

Before we begin our investigation into the location of the lost Ark of the Covenant we have to ask one question: Has any evidence been found for the Ark's existence? Unfortunately for archaeologists there is no easy answer to this question. The proposed site of Solomon's Temple in Jerusalem, where the Ark resided, is currently occupied by the Dome of the Rock Shrine and archaeological exploration is forbidden on the grounds of political and religious claims. A great deal of construction work has been carried out on the Temple Mount and there have been reports from conscientious Arabs that ancient Hebrew texts have been found and destroyed. These accounts are difficult to substantiate, for no-one wants to be identified as a traitor to the Arabs. Nevertheless, the Temple Mount Salvage Operation is sifting through the 'rubbish' that was dug up and dumped by the authorities working on the Temple Mount, and they have recovered artefacts dating back to the First Temple period and arrow heads from the time of the Babylonian invasion of Judah! We now have archaeological evidence that proves the Babylonians were fighting on the Temple Mount as the Bible describes and it was at this time that the Ark was lost. Anyhow, as excavations are not permitted on the Temple Mount to search for Solomon's Temple, or the resting place of the Ark, we can only begin our search by considering just two artefacts, out of many, which collaborates biblical history.

As you know, in our last investigation we examined the case for the Hebrew exodus out of Egypt. In this process we came to the Temple of Pharaoh Merneptah, where we saw the Merneptah Stela, a 3,200 year old stone containing the first record of Israel outside of the Bible! This

stela proves beyond all contradiction, that several hundred years before the Bible indicates that Solomon built a Temple in Jerusalem, an ancient people called Israel were living in the land of Canaan.

The second artefact that we must consider is the Tel Dan Stele, dating roughly to 850 years before Christ. This Aramaic inscription includes 'Israel' and the 'House of David.' This is the first reference to the Kingdom of David outside of the Bible, approximately 120 years after his death. This stone indicates that the surrounding kingdoms recognised Israel as a nation and acknowledged that David was the founder of a dynasty of rulers. We do not have any evidence that Israel had the Ark of the Covenant in their possession, but with these inscriptions confirming the biblical

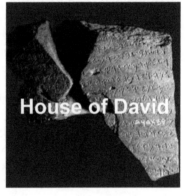

account, we do not need to take a great leap of faith to believe that these people did indeed produce and revere a golden chest, which contained their law.

According to the Bible, it was in the region of the Sinai Peninsula that the Ark of the Covenant was conceived and made. Somewhere in this vast desert, the holiest object in world history was born.

But what did the Ark look like? From the Bible's book of Exodus, we learn that God instructed Moses at Mount Sinai to build a sacred wooden container to hold the two tablets of the covenant made between God and His people. This wooden chest, called the Ark of the Covenant was made out of acacia wood, and was overlaid inside and out with gold. It was almost four feet long and just over two feet wide and high, with a mercy seat and two cherubim on top. We learn from Exodus 37:1 that Moses commissioned a skilled man named Bezalel to make the Ark within specific guidelines.

The Ark of the Covenant held the sacred laws of God and it was symbolic of God's relationship with His people. To understand the importance of the Ark to ancient Israel, we must first be aware that it was conceived on the mountain of the Lord during a powerful revelation of God's holiness, judgment, glory and might. 'Now Mount Sinai was completely in smoke, because the Lord had descended upon it in fire...and the whole mountain quaked greatly...Now all the people witnessed the thunderings, the lightning flashes...and they trembled and stood afar off' Exodus 19:18, 20:18.

When God revealed Himself to Israel, His potent manifestation made the people tremble in holy fear. The first revelation of God to Israel was overwhelming. The message to His chosen nation was distinct. God is Almighty, He is holy and sinful mankind dare not come near Him, Exodus 19:21. The design for the Ark of the Covenant was given at this time, and as a consequence the Ark was a practical demonstration of the separation between God and man. How could a holy God abide with the sinful people of Israel?

On the sacred mountain, orders were also given for the design of the Tabernacle, the forerunner to Solomon's Temple. This large tent was made for religious ceremonies and was separated into special areas, with the Holy of Holies closed off to almost everyone. It was in this hallowed section of the Holiest of All that the Ark was to rest. "Then you shall bring the Ark of the Testimony in there, behind the veil. The veil shall be a divider for you, between the holy place and the Most Holy" Exodus 26:33.

The New Testament explains that God used the design of the Tabernacle to unveil the mystery of His plan for mankind's redemption. 'Into the second part (of the Tabernacle) the high priest went alone once a year, not without blood, which he offered for himself and for the people's sins...The Holy Spirit indicating this, that the way into the Holiest of All (heaven) was not yet manifest while the first Tabernacle was still standing' Hebrews 9:7-8.

Kept inside the Ark were the two tablets of the Testimony of God's covenant with Israel, the golden pot containing the manna which the Israelites ate in the wilderness and Aaron's rod, Hebrews 9:4. On the outside of the Ark, two poles made out of acacia wood were held in place by golden rings and only the Levites were allowed to carry the Ark in the prescribed manner. Those who ignored the sacred precepts for carrying it were struck dead, 2 Samuel 6:6-7. Hollywood and some authors have indicated that the Ark had some mystical power, but the Bible verifies that when Israel put her faith in the Ark, rather than the Lord, they forfeited God's protection and were defeated by their enemies, 1 Samuel 4:5-10. Yet, ancient Israel did take the Ark with them into battle and it symbolised God's presence among them, fighting on their behalf, Joshua 6:6-8. When the Ark was carried it had to be covered with a veil, badger skins and a blue cloth. The people were not to see the Ark, Numbers 4:5-6. Finally, the Ark was designed by God to be the place where He spoke with the leaders of His people. "I will speak with you from above the mercy seat, from between the two cherubim which are on the Ark of the Testimony" Exodus 25:22.

The Burning Bush

'The Angel of the Lord appeared to him in a flame of fire from the midst of a bush' Exodus 3:2.

In our last investigation, we learnt that no-one has proved conclusively where Mount Sinai is located. Yet we did confirm that it is not situated in the currently favoured location of Saudi Arabia. When Paul wrote that Mount Sinai is in Arabia, he was using the Roman understanding of this expression, which included the Sinai Peninsula, Galatians 4:25. He was not using a twenty-first century map and pointing out Saudi Arabia. The text in Exodus 18 leaves no doubt that the mountain of God is not in Saudi Arabia. Moses' father-in-law left his home in Midian (Saudi Arabia) and met Moses at Mount Sinai, Exodus 18:1-6, 27. Later, 'Moses let his father-in-law depart (from Mount Sinai) and he went his way to his own land' (Saudi Arabia). In Numbers 10:29-33, Moses' father-in-law confirms again that Mount Sinai is not in Midian by stating on this second occasion at the mountain, "I will depart to my own land."

With this in mind, we visited the traditional site of Mount Sinai to aid our understanding of the terrain where the Ark of the Covenant was crafted into existence, Exodus 36-40. When we entered Saint Katherine's Monastery, we rapidly came to appreciate that the thin line between legend and historical fact can be blurred with ease.

The priests stated without any reservation, that the bush which was draping down into the courtyard was indeed the same burning bush that Moses had seen! This monastery has a very prestigious heritage, therefore it was a shame to overstep the mark into fiction. However, the experience at the real burning bush transformed Moses' life from a shepherd living a quiet life, to a spiritual leader that led Israel out of Egypt, to the desert where the Ark was made.

This wonderful religious residence at the base of the traditional site of Mount Sinai is one of the oldest Christian monasteries in the world. It is the home of ancient copies of the Scriptures, priceless art and a Christian witness that has lasted for over one and a half millennia. We were hoping to find some inspiration for our quest for the Ark of the Covenant, but there were no leads, so our mission took us onward through the Sinai Peninsula and towards Alexandria. Would we find any clues in that renowned ancient city?

The City under the Sea
'A certain Jew named Apollos, born at Alexandria
...and mighty in the Scriptures' Acts 18:24.

After a lengthy drive we arrived in Alexandria, the city that launched a thousand legends. Cleopatra's palace once stood here; she was the last pharaoh of Egypt and when she died, ancient Egypt was soon buried with her. Thousands of years of history came crashing to the ground with her last breath, as Egypt became just another province in the Roman Empire. Alexander the Great founded this city and it boasted an ancient wonder. The lighthouse of Alexandria was one of the seven wonders of the ancient world and it was the first sight ships would see as they came close to port. When ships docked they were searched for books which were copied for the greatest library of the ancient world. The old library, whose precise location is unknown, would have stored an ancient copy of the Torah. In Alexandria, there was a large Jewish community and it was in this city that the Hebrew Bible was translated into Greek. In consequence could we learn anything about the Ark here? We spent some time in the new library, with no success. After the library, we examined the ancient sites and artefacts of Alexandria. We found items from the Egyptian, Greek and Roman periods, and biblical manuscripts from the early Christian era, but no clues to the Ark.

Little remains of ancient Alexandria, but her history is extraordinary; in the early Christian era it was the residence for the first missionary school and it was a major port. This centre is also famed for being a genuine city under the sea! The myths of sunken cities have captivated many imaginations, yet we discovered that parts of this metropolis are still lost under water. Once a diver was in the bay of Alexandria and out of the watery haze he saw the face of a pharaoh looking directly at him! Alexandria suffered from earthquakes and subsidence that forced parts of the ancient city to sink into the sea. In the bay today are the remains of Cleopatra's palace and the great lighthouse. Some of the city's relics have now been brought to the surface and rest in the Open Air Museum, by the Roman Coliseum.

Excavations at Alexandria still continue, but the trail for the Ark of the Covenant had gone cold. So it was expedient for us to travel back into the relics of the New Kingdom of ancient Egypt and enter the tomb of the world's most famous pharaoh to search for leads.

Tutankhamun's Gold
'The treasures of gold and silver...all the precious things of Egypt' Daniel 11:43.

When we entered Tutankhamun's tomb in the Valley of the Kings, in Luxor, we were astonished at how little this sepulchre is. Compared to many other tombs, the primary chamber is about the size of a garage. Pharaoh Tutankhamun was only a teenager when he died and with over three hundred pharaohs in Egyptian history, he was quickly forgotten by most. In fact, his low profile in Egyptian history is the reason why the antiquities of his tomb were kept safely buried underground; the thieves forgot about this insignificant pharaoh! Beyond the entrance corridor, this world famous tomb has four main chambers - of critical value to us were the burial chamber and the treasury. The intact tomb of Tutankhamun was discovered in 1922, after years of diligent excavation by the archaeologist Howard Carter. The golden treasures found inside are now on display in the Egyptian Museum. Visitors rush to see his famous golden facemask, but the antiquity that caught our eyes was the Portable Simulacrum of Anubis, for its similarity to the Bible's Ark of the Covenant! With a little computer cultivation, we saw how this gold plated wooden box could be transformed! First remove the doglike Anubis, then overlay the worn Egyptian golden symbols with a golden covering and finally add an artist's impression of the two cherubim.

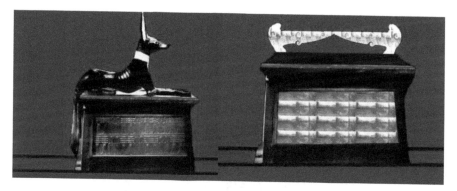

Moses was trained in ancient Egypt and Tutankhamun's funeral hoard proves that sacred boxes, covered with gold and carried with poles were familiar to Egyptians. As we established what the Ark's literal image may have looked like, we had to proceed to examine the historical record to find out what happened to the Ark, and ask if it still exists, after over three millennia since its creation.

KV62: Tutankhamun's Tomb

Burial Chamber   Treasury

Antechamber

Annexe

Corridor

If our inquiry is to detect what happened to the Ark of the Covenant, we must ask when was the last time articles from the Temple of Jerusalem were seen and visually recorded for posterity? To do this, we must look back many years to our travels to Rome, Italy. The great coliseum in Rome is spectacular, yet how many people know that it was partly funded by the destruction of Judea?

In 70 AD, Titus with his father's blessing completed his objective to take Jerusalem; the Temple was destroyed and the sacred artefacts inside were stolen. Jesus' prophecy had come true, Matthew 24:2. Many Jews were sold as slaves and profit from this campaign helped pay for the coliseum. Titus catalogued his war on a triumphal arch in Rome and his memorial contains an incredible depiction.

This is the equivalent of a two thousand year old photo of the sacred biblical treasures from the Temple which Jesus once preached in, Ezra 6:5, Matthew 21:12. Clearly visible is the seven-branched golden menorah, the silver trumpets and possibly the jewel covered table of Divine Presence, Exodus 25:31-32, Ezra 3:10, Hebrews 9.

Almost two millennia later, this monument allows us to look inside the Holy Temple of Jerusalem and see the objects that are listed in the Bible! The Romans took the Temple treasure to their capital and this record proves beyond contradiction that the articles mentioned in the Bible were verifiable objects. This incredible chronicle is the closest we can get to literally seeing inside Jerusalem's Temple! Conspicuously absent from the memorial is the Ark. This chronicle therefore indicates the Ark was never captured by Rome and scholars agree with considerable certainty that the Ark was never in the Second Temple. But what happened to these Jewish treasures?

It is estimated that Vespasian looted fifty tons of gold from the Jews; much of this was used to pay for building projects and soldiers; but the vessels from Herod's Temple were publicly displayed and later stored. Josephus wrote in the first century that Vespasian erected a Temple of Peace in Rome and inside 'he laid up the vessels of gold from the Temple of the Jews.' In 455 AD, Rome was looted by the Vandals, their temples were emptied and ships sailed to Carthage (Tunisia) with the booty. Almost eighty years later, the Byzantine Emperor Justinian defeated the Vandals, bringing back glory to the new Roman Empire. He also brought back the treasure of the Jews; for Procopius chronicled that in Constantinople these vessels were displayed including 'the treasures of the Jews, which Titus, the son of Vespasian... had brought to Rome after the capture of Jerusalem.'

The emperor Justinian had some form of Christian faith and a fear of God to go with it. Procopius attests that a Jew in his court saw the Temple vessels and said, "These treasures, I think it inexpedient (a mistake) to carry them into the palace of Byzantium. Indeed it is not possible for them to be elsewhere than in the place where Solomon, the King of the Jews formerly placed them." Then he warned Justinian that every empire which held these treasures soon fell. In fear of offending God Justinian 'sent everything to the sanctuary of the Christians in Jerusalem.' The Church of the Holy Sepulchre was the most prestigious, so if this account can be trusted, the Second Temple vessels arrived back in Jerusalem around 550 AD. Just over six decades later, in 614 AD, Persian armies invaded Jerusalem and a document called *The Khuzistan Chronicle* details that thieves dug into the Church of the Holy Sepulchre looking for the articles, but did not find them. The Second Temple treasures had disappeared. Since then many have proposed locations, churches, monasteries and empires that took the vessels, but no genuine leads have been forthcoming. Some believe that the coming Islamic conquests led to them being melted down, others state that they are locked inside the Vatican vaults and in 1996 Israel's Religious Affairs Minister officially asked for their return. The Vatican denied ever possessing them. On a positive note, these chronicles and the Scriptures indicate that in antiquity, the victors of wars paraded the captured treasures of other peoples and stored them in a splurge of self-indulgence. This gives us hope that the Ark of the Covenant, if ever captured, was not dismantled and melted down for its gold. Could it still be out there?

In the time of Solomon, a Temple was erected in ancient Israel to be a permanent residence for the Ark of the Covenant, 1 Kings 5-8; but five years after Solomon's death, the Bible chronicles that the Temple was raided by Pharaoh Shishak. If we can find the Egyptian account of this campaign, perhaps we can find some clues to discover what happened to the lost golden and silver treasures from Solomon's Temple.

We hired some bikes for the day, to give us access to places off the tourist routes and our intention paid dividends. As we cycled, we noticed Egyptian relics and broken sphinxes on the waste ground, away from the road. We followed these splintered remains, until we turned a corner to find an ancient paved road, with an avenue of sphinxes stationed on both sides as far as the eye could see. We were far away from the main tourist entrance to the Temple of Karnack and this avenue was quiet, almost abandoned. We anticipated seeing groups of tourists around the corner, yet instead we found another empty road, leading to a large temple entrance. We had literally stumbled upon this almost abandoned entrance to the Karnack complex and we

felt like one of the first explorers, who by accident had found a lost temple. These sphinxes once joined the Temple of Luxor in the centre of town, to the very large Temple of Karnack and it was these dilapidated remains which we had unintentionally followed.

The Bible immortalises in the sacred text that a pharaoh called Shishak invaded Judah and took away the treasures of Solomon's Temple. In our research we identified that Shishak is the Hebrew translation of the name Sheshonq. Consequently in the Temple of Karnack we scoured for any references to or by Pharaoh Sheshonq I. Then in an incredible confirmation of Scripture, we found the story of Egypt's invasion of the land of Canaan on a wall in this temple!

Though this relief is gravely damaged, its original intent was to represent Pharaoh Sheshonq I and the god Amun taking captive the enemies of Egypt.

By studying this Egyptian record of the campaign of Sheshonq I, Egyptologists have been able to use this data to draw up a possible route which this pharaoh may have taken. Several of the places identified on the wall can still be found today, yet lamentably many names have been badly damaged and are now unreadable. Jerusalem is missing from the wall, but the route indicates it was on the itinerary as the Bible confirms.

Evidence for this campaign has also been traced on an Egyptian relief in Megiddo, Israel. Having identified confirmation of the Bible's description of Shishak's invasion, we wondered if it would be possible to find what this man did with Solomon's treasures.

Could it be possible to track down the gold and silver that came from Solomon's Temple? Could you imagine seeing the wealth that once rested inside Israel's first Temple! This was a captivating concept.

When Solomon reigned, the Bible indicates that Israel arrived at its greatest peak, with mountains of wealth and an empire. During the same time, Egypt was in a long period of decline, for the glory days of the New Kingdom were far behind and Egypt was struggling in their Third Intermediate Period. Plunder became more important to the weakened Egypt and the Bible states that the fame of Solomon's wealth had spread throughout the world, 1 Kings 10, 2 Chronicles 12:9. Between these two nations, the small and wealthy Israel and the inadequate Egypt entered Jeroboam. In his pride, Solomon had forsaken the Lord, and a prophet told Jeroboam that the nation of Israel would be divided and he would lead ten tribes. Upon hearing this Solomon sought to kill Jeroboam and he fled to Pharaoh Shishak in Egypt, 1 Kings 11:29-40. No doubt the tidings of political instability in Israel were great news for Shishak because there was a great deal of wealth in Jerusalem. Jewish experts who have studied the wealth of Israel during the age of David and Solomon have summarised that the Bible describes them having many thousands of tons of gold and silver, 1 Kings 6-7, 1 Chronicles 28 and 29, 2 Chronicles 2-4. When scholars question the Bible's account, commentators call attention to Alexander the Great who took huge amounts of gold from ancient kingdoms in his campaigns.

After Solomon's death, Jeroboam left Egypt and returned to Israel to present the case for a tax cut for the people, after the late king's expensive building campaigns. The new king ignored the plea and alienated his people, causing the split of the Kingdom into Israel and Judah, 1 Kings 11:29-12:19. This division fundamentally weakened the capacity of the Jews to defend themselves from any military threat. Meanwhile, the wealth of the Jews was tantalising for any foreign power and Shishak's war machine was soon entering the land. Every pharaoh needed a successful military campaign to boost their support at home and plunder from foreign people would help to pacify Egypt's troubles.

Some scholars believe that Judah was so weak that they could not fight and they gave Shishak Solomon's treasures to save the Temple. But where did he take their riches?

The next phase in our investigation was to travel to Tanis, the city where Shishak launched his attack on Judah and the place where his sons were buried. However, could archaeologists ever find any gold or silver here? Grave robbers are sometimes as infamous as the pharaohs, for they managed to search out and empty the royal tombs of their wealth. In fact, the situation was so bad that Egyptian priests eventually gathered and hid away the mummified bodies of their pharaohs in order to protect them. Pharaoh Shishak's tomb and the wealth within have never been found. No leads there then. Nevertheless in Tanis riches were uncovered second only to Tutankhamun's; yet the discovery was never made famous for this excavation took place during WWII, when the world had bigger problems to think about and the finds were only published in French.

Tanis was the burial ground for the successors of the pharaoh who attacked Jerusalem and just fifty years after his death, Pharaoh Osorkon II came to power. We entered his tomb, with many others besides and we chanced upon a window into the ancient world.

The Bible declares that Shishak took the wealth of Jerusalem and Egyptians were always working on projects, including burial deposits which needed gold and silver. Therefore was any of Solomon's treasure melted down and recast to be buried in these royal tombs? Many of the antiquities of Jerusalem were taken by Shishak and when archaeologists excavated these tombs, they identified golden treasures that the grave robbers had missed. Inside they dug up a bracelet bearing the name of Sheshonq I, the man who took Judah's wealth and his relatives were buried with gold and silver. Sheshonq II had a golden face mask and a large silver coffin. When Solomon reigned he boasted of the abundance of silver in Jerusalem, but after his death Egypt plundered the nation, 2 Chronicles 9:10-27.

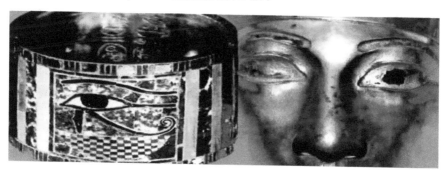

Our next stop was at the Egyptian Museum the new home of these relics which were buried for over two and half millennia. In the Tanis exhibit, next to Tutankhamun's display, we stood speechless gazing at the bracelet worn by the pharaoh who entered Jerusalem and took the wealth from Israel's first Temple! How many Christians visit this museum without realising that the man who wore this bracelet saw Solomon's Temple? Two steps away, we found the silver coffin and the golden facemask. These discoveries are almost unknown to the public and whilst experts cannot prove that these antiquities were made with Jerusalem's wealth, the link remains provocative.

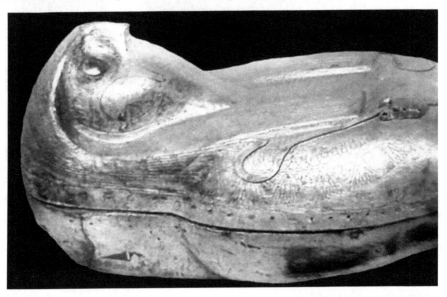

When we ask what happened to the wealth of Solomon's Temple, the Bible gives us the answer. One of the culprits who stripped the Temple was Shishak, and plunder from his campaign would have been used to build his memorial in the Temple of Karnack, whilst some of Jerusalem's gold and silver may have been recast, and buried in Tanis. But did Shishak take the Ark of the Covenant? The Bible chronicles that he took many Temple articles, yet it suggests that other holy items must have been left, with the Ark itself being one such object, 2 Kings 24:13-14, 25:8-17. For the priests of Jerusalem the Ark of the Covenant and other sacred items were not pawns to be traded in for a short-term peace - the Ark was where God Himself dwelt, Leviticus 16:2, Num. 7:89. Also, the Bible confirms that the Ark did not go with Shishak, for it records the Ark being in Jerusalem many centuries later, 2 Chronicles 35:3. Therefore Egypt's Shishak did not gain possession of the Ark of the Covenant.

In our last investigation to find the exodus evidence, we learnt that Egypt acknowledged the existence of the ancient people of Israel 1,200 years before Christ. Sheshonq's report of the invasion of the land combined with the Bible's account communicates once again that Egyptians and the people of the Bible coexisted in the ancient world of historical fact. However, in all of Egypt's chronicles we have only been able to find one direct reference to the name Israel. This conundrum presents the sincere possibility that Israel and Judah may have been cited many times in Egyptian history using a generic name for Semitic people, and it could also indicate that Egyptians used another name for the Jews which is still unknown.

The Bible and Egyptian history agree that Shishak invaded the land, yet in the Egyptian narrative we do not find the name Israel or Judah. For the Jews, the invasion of the land was a traumatic event worthy of note, but for the Egyptians God's people were just one of many weaker kingdoms that needed to be put in their place. Unfortunately, the relief of Shishak's invasion is terribly damaged, to the extent that the depiction of this pharaoh has been destroyed. Therefore, it could be the case that Judah and Jerusalem were mentioned directly in the substantial areas of this damage relief. Yet we are fortunate that this memorial of Shishak's war stands as another incredible confirmation of the accuracy of biblical history.

Nonetheless, it is still a mystery why Egyptian history proves they acknowledged the existence of the people of Israel in the land for over 1,200 years and still in all of that time, they chose only once to directly indicate their presence! Some have proposed this was a political ploy by the Egyptians. For ancient Egypt, the land of Canaan was their area of influence, often within Egypt's direct control. This land was their colony, part of their empire and the Bible's description of the Jewish presence in the land appears to confirm that for most of their existence, God's people were pawns in the game of other powers. Therefore, the suggestion has been made that by refusing to directly acknowledge the Kingdom of Israel and Judah, Egypt was reassessing its claim to Canaan. Perhaps we can hear their empire builders stating, "The

Kingdoms of Israel and Judah do not exist; only Egypt's right to the land exists." Three and a half millennia later, most of the neighbours of modern Israel still apply this method to disenfranchise the Jews.

The ancient Hebrews throughout much of their history were effectively second-class citizens in their own nation, and other empires made them realise they were the weak subjects of foreign powers, in a land which they had claimed for their own.

We don't sufficiently understand why the Ancient Egyptians made only one direct reference to the people of Israel and their descendants, but we can confirm that for over one thousand years, the nation of Egypt knew that a people called Israel were living in the land. Also, in the case of Shishak and other biblical events Egypt's chronicle adds credence to the valid Scriptural narrative. There may be more details of the Jews to be detected in Egyptian accounts and with three millennia passing, some of these may have been destroyed. Fortunately, we do have the records of many other peoples and nations, who recognised and immortalised the existence of the people of the Bible in their reliefs.

The Bible specifically states that God made the Jews the servants of Pharaoh Shishak in order to teach them the difference between serving a foreign power, to serving Him faithfully, 2 Chronicles 12:8. This lesson should have taught them that it is better to be righteous, faithful to the Lord and free, rather than being wicked, backslidden and a slave to a foreign power. However, the people of the Bible failed to listen to their prophets and refused spiritual instruction.

Ancient Egypt was a major player in the story of Israel, yet as with all the great civilisations, it declined as other powers arose. We arrived in the Valley of the Queens in Luxor, to enter a new set of tombs. In this area many powerful people were buried who saw Egypt's finest hour, but also others witnessed the long period of decline that led to Egypt's retreat from Canaan. The long heyday of Egypt changed history, but as it weakened, other nations both great and small, quickly became a threat to Israel and Judah. The Bible documents that Solomon's Temple, the home of the Ark, was plundered many times by these peoples and by studying the Bible we can learn what happened to Solomon's treasures. The Scriptures bear witness that articles from Jerusalem were taken to Egypt, (1 Kings 14:25-26), Syria (1 Kings 15:18, 2 Kings 12:18, 2 Chronicles 16:2), Assyria (2 Kings 16:8, 17-20, 18:15), Arabia, (2 Chronicles 21:16-17), Babylon (2 Kings 24:13-14, 25:8-19, 2 Chronicles 36:10,18, Daniel 1:2), Sidon, Tyre, Philistia (Joel 3:4-5) and woefully the King of Israel plundered the Temple (2 Kings 14:12-14, 2 Chronicles 25:22-24). Nevertheless, none of these biblical accounts record that the Ark was taken.

When Egypt was deteriorating as a power, the Bible announced the rise of the Assyrian threat to Judah and Israel, 2 Chronicles 32, and in an astonishing validation of biblical history an Assyrian relief confirms these events and gives us the only representation of a King of Israel! This is Jehu King of Israel, anointed by the prophet Elijah and according

to the Bible made subject to Assyria because of Israel's sins, 1 Kings 19. 'But Jehu took no heed to walk in the law of the Lord God of Israel' 2 Kings 10:31. This Black Obelisk affirms the Bible's account of ancient history, and there are many other artefacts that support the Bible's description of the following years - including the Babylonian Chronicle of Years 605-594 B.C. which validates that Assyria was later surpassed by Babylon and

that Judah was invaded by the Babylonians, 2 Kings 24, 2 Chronicles 36, Daniel 1. The Bible states that 'Nebuchadnezzar King of Babylon came against the city' of Jerusalem, 2 Kings 24:11. 'Then they burned down the house of God...and the treasures...he took to Babylon' 2 Chronicles 36:18-19. Jeremiah the prophet lived through these days and just before the Babylonian invasion his chronicle indicates that the Ark of the Covenant was still in Jerusalem, Jeremiah 3:16. Nevertheless, in 586 B.C., Solomon's Temple was destroyed by the Babylonians and the Ark of the Covenant disappeared from the pages of history.

Jeremiah registered that many Jews escaped into Egypt at this time and some believe that the Ark of the Covenant left Jerusalem for safety in Egypt, just before the fall of King Solomon's Temple, Jeremiah 42-46. But where did these Jews go in Egypt? Are there any

Jewish settlements in Egypt where they could have fled?

We studied the Scriptures to learn where the Jews lived in Egypt and we found that Isaiah wrote that in his lifetime many Jews were already settled in Sinim, which is an area around Aswan, Isaiah 49:12. Did the fleeing Jews come here? In Aswan, we looked for any leads to help us

find the evidence for an ancient Jewish community being near. We visited the tombs of the Nobles, overlooking Aswan, but we detected nothing helpful, so we hired a boat to sail on the Nile. As we sailed on the river, our eyes were drawn sumptuously toward Elephantine Island and it was on this very settlement that a very exciting discovery was made. Archaeologists uncovered a large collection of ancient Jewish manuscripts dating to around 500 years before Christ, proving that a Jewish community once lived at this site.

To the amazement of many, a letter called the Petition to Bagoas confirmed that a Jewish temple once stood on this island in Egypt! The letter stated it was called the Temple of Yahweh and the Passover Letter certified that the priests carried out animal and grain sacrifices, whilst observing the Passover as Moses instructed. Using the data available from the archaeological remains at the site, we constructed an artist's impression of this Jewish temple.

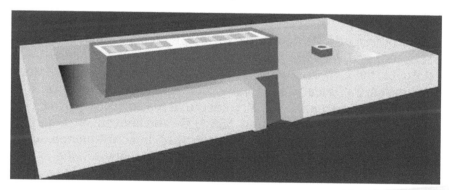

Why was there a Jewish temple in Egypt? The Bible indicates that the primary purpose for building the original temple was to house the Ark of the Covenant, so was this temple built for the same purpose? 1 Chronicles 17:1. When Jewish scholars examined the remains of this temple, they discovered it was very similar in size to the Tabernacle of Moses, and this was never designed to be the final resting place for the Ark of the Covenant. Instead the Ark stayed in the Tabernacle whilst God's people hoped for a permanent sanctuary to be built in their land, Deuteronomy 12:11,14. We also determined from these letters that this Jewish community was in contact with the captives who were returning after the exile to Jerusalem, for they note Johanan a Levite and Sanballat; both men are cited in the Bible, Nehemiah 2:19, 12:23. Consequently, this provides independent verification of the Bible's account of these characters!

Jeremiah prophesied trouble for the Jews in Egypt and the Petition to Bagoas confirmed that disorder did come, for the temple was 'burned to the ground…in the fourteenth year of Darius,' and, 'as for the basins of gold and silver and other articles that were in the temple' the Egyptians 'carried all of them off' Jeremiah 44:13-14. It's not possible to prove the Ark was once in this lost Jewish temple, but if the Levite priests did flee Jerusalem to keep the Ark safe, then this is the only location that meets the biblical requirements for its safe keeping. Secondly, its presence would compare favourable with legends that the Ark was taken south for its own safety.

If the Ark formerly resided in this temple, it had to be moved before its destruction, and we were told that because of the turmoil in Jerusalem and Egypt, the only safe place for the Ark was south, with the Jewish communities in Africa, Zephaniah 3:10, Acts 8:27. Therefore, if this temple was used to keep the Ark secure, it would have arrived before the fall of Solomon's Temple in 586 B.C. and moved on before 407 B.C., when this Jewish temple was destroyed. In consequence, we had to study the Bible and Egyptian chronicles to find any Kingdoms south of Egypt where the Ark may have gone.

Pharaoh Hatshepsut's Mission to Africa
'A man of Ethiopia...of great authority...had come to Jerusalem to worship' Acts 8:27.

The Bible unveils there were numerous great African Kingdoms in the ancient world; sadly many were lost in the sands of time. Thus we went to Hatshepsut's Temple in Luxor, to evaluate Egypt's greatest relief of a lost African Kingdom, 2 Kings 19:9, 2 Chronicles 14:9. In this temple the female Pharaoh Hatshepsut details a historic expedition on the Red Sea to a land she called Punt. Stepping back around 3,500 years, these carvings allow us to visualise a lost African Kingdom! These depictions even portray an image of a leader of this forgotten African land, calling her Queen Ity.

Egyptian reliefs of the land of Punt exemplify the types of homes that these Africans resided in over three millennia ago. Who were the people that lived in these dwellings and where was this land located? Pharaoh Hatshepsut took seven great ships to the land of Punt, to bring back incense trees and other precious items. These illustrations indicate it was a large trading venture and as we examined them, we realised these records were consistent with the Bible's account of the Kingdom of Sheba.

Hundreds of years after this trip, the Queen of Sheba, who came from a land south of Israel, visited Solomon and they exchanged gifts like those engraved here, Luke 11:31. The Bible divulges that the Queen of Sheba gave Solomon 'gold, spices in great quantity and precious stones' 1 Kings 10:10. Experts who have studied the Bible's account of the land of Sheba have concluded there are two primary locations where it could have been located. One is in the region of Yemen, the other is the horn of Africa in or by Ethiopia. Those who have studied this region became aware that the empires based in this part of the world have ruled parts of Yemen and Ethiopia at the same time. Could this be the Bible's land of Sheba? Jesus Himself indicated that Sheba was a land very far away and was south of Israel saying, "The Queen of the south...came from the ends of the earth to hear the wisdom of Solomon" Matthew 12:42.

As we pondered these matters, we discovered that some scholars have identified that the descriptions of the land of Punt and Sheba are both consistent with the nation of Ethiopia. This theory suggests that hundreds of years after the Egyptian visit to the land of Punt, the nation evolved into the kingdom of Sheba. This concept was very interesting to us, because millions of people believe a legend that the Ark of the Covenant was smuggled by Levite priests into Ethiopia around the time of the Queen of Sheba.

Are these stories which we heard serious historical accounts or just myths? Our mission was to investigate these leads to discover if they had any basis in fact. To do this, we had to sail up the River Nile into Sudan and cross the desert into Ethiopia.

Egypt, Sudan and Ethiopia
'Fear not, for I am with you. Be not dismayed, for I am your God' Isaiah 41:10.

We queued up at the ferry port, the only one between Egypt and Sudan and saw a scene that you would expect to witness in a film set in the nineteenth century. Hundreds of people were crowded around, shouting in various languages, with large packages and containers on their heads. There was a rush for tickets and traders ran onto the ship, hoping to find any space for their goods before it was full. On the slope before the ferry, a man lost control of his heavy laden two wheeled cart and chased it as it ploughed towards the crowd below.

Eight hours later, we were still docked, with boxes, barrels and an unknown quantity of goods bursting from every space. We walked around the deck and witnessed that ninety-eight percent of the passengers were locals. There was a good reason why tourists weren't planning their holiday in the Sudan. Just a few months before an English teacher was arrested for a perceived insult to Islam and the extremists called for her to be beheaded. Only careful negotiation by the moderates secured her release. With this story still fresh in our minds from the news, we went to sleep as we sailed towards the border.

In the morning, we awoke still in Egyptian waters. On the deck we saw our last glimpse of Egypt, as we sailed past the four statues of Ramesses II at Abu-Simbel, the historic boundary between ancient Egypt and the Nubian Kingdom. Several hours later we came close to the border and everybody on deck was forced to go inside as a Sudanese boat was on its way to inspect us. Out of the distance, a vessel with armed guards onboard sped towards us and landed. The atmosphere felt very tense and we wondered if we had made a mistake in coming. A few hours later, we docked and took our first look out of the window. We saw a guard, wearing blacked out glasses and a hardened stare on his face. Fortunately, our cloak and dagger ordeal transformed as a friendly team of bureaucrats arrived onboard to check the passports of the few foreigners, and led us to a four-wheeled vehicle that sped through the dust into a settlement. That night we slept in a sandy ghost-community in the desert and awoke for the two day train ride on a hard seat to Khartoum. In the capital, we had to register with the government as foreigners and paid a large fee for the pleasure.

Five days later, we were in a small vehicle leaving the nation with many locals, and at a checkpoint one woman had faulty documents and she was removed. We then crossed with some relief out of Sudan and into Ethiopia. On the border, no-one spoke English, but the kind locals directed us to a small hut where eight of us slept. We were on the trail of the Ark and it was taking us into the unknown!

The Bible illustrates that there was a large Jewish community in Ethiopia long before the time of Christ. We cannot confirm where the borders of Ethiopia were in those days, as they are subject to change; nonetheless it is evident that this Jewish tradition can still be observed in Ethiopia today. The New Testament also confirms that practising Jews were in prominent positions in Ethiopia and that Ethiopian Jews began to embrace Christ as Messiah, Acts 8:27.

Ethiopia is the land of lost civilisations, mentioned in the Bible, recorded in ancient literature and re-discovered by archaeologists. Yet of all the mysteries of this land, only one tale takes us back to the story of the lost Ark of the Covenant. As we questioned the Ethiopians about it, they told us with certainty that Ethiopia gained possession of the Ark several millennia ago. If their claim is true, how did they get it? Our first thought was of the Jewish temple that we found in Elephantine, Egypt. Did Levite priests take the Ark from that temple and smuggle it into Ethiopia during that era of war and crisis? However, the Ethiopians alleged they had the Ark of the Covenant a long time before the construction of that temple. In fact, their claim goes all the way back to the time of Solomon! We knew that we needed to find an original source document to confirm what and why the Ethiopians believe these things, so after doing some research, we realised we needed to find an ancient book called the *Kebra Nagast* - Ethiopia's book of the Glory of Kings. We wanted to examine the oldest surviving copy available; but

lamentably a fire had devastated the aged monastery containing these; so we came to the third highest capital in the world, Addis Ababa, to inspect an old rock church, located at the highest peak of the capital.

We hired a taxi to go to the church on Mount Entoto, but the elevation led it to overheat and after a few hours of breakdowns, we arrived and arranged to see the famous *Kebra Nagast*.

According to this book, after the Queen of Sheba visited Solomon in Israel, she returned back to Ethiopia to find she was pregnant with his son. Years later the child called Menelik, went to Israel to see his father and after witnessing the backsliding of Solomon, he left under the cover of darkness taking the Ark of the Covenant with him to Ethiopia, where it still resides today! Immediately we sensed some inconsistencies with this story and as this legend is not found in the Bible, it needs to be tested thoroughly. It would be easy to quickly dismiss this Ethiopian claim because of the contradictions we found, however we must recall that this is the only nation on earth that has a religion which is still centred on the Ark of the Covenant. Every Ethiopian Orthodox church possesses a replica of the Ark in a part of their sanctuary which they call the Holy of Holies, and it is central to their worship. These facts imply that at some point in history the Ethiopians obtained 'an Ark', but was it 'the Ark?'

After pondering this, our immediate hypothesis was that the Ethiopian Ark of the Covenant could have arrived from four sources. 1. Levite priests from the temple of Elephantine in Egypt smuggled the Ark from

their temple to this nation. 2. An Ethiopian emperor had a replica Ark made and alleged it to be real, to substantiate his claim to the throne. 3. The Jewish communities in Ethiopia built an Ark, as they were unable to worship back in Jerusalem. 4. The Ethiopian legend of the Queen of Sheba's son bringing the original Ark to this nation has validity.

We also visited many other churches in Addis Ababa, including this one to view other copies of their holy book. In every church and city we found that the Ethiopian Christians believed in Sheba's legend. However, the account of her having a son with Solomon and the Ark being brought into this nation is not found in the Bible. Therefore we had to examine these legends by visiting the remains of the ancient and forgotten civilisations of Ethiopia!

Underground Rock Churches
'From beyond the rivers of Ethiopia, My worshippers, the daughter of My dispersed ones (the Jews), shall bring My offering' Zep. 3:10.

Our mission to find the forgotten and overlooked Ethiopia began at Gondar, where we discovered buildings that we never imagined we would find in this nation. This is Africa's Camelot, which dates to the sixteen hundreds and these castles echo Ethiopia's Christian and Jewish heritage. As we explored them, we found many references in the architecture to Ethiopia's biblical aspirations, but if we were to examine the legend of the regal Queen of Sheba, we would need to go back further in time. Our next

stop led us back almost one millennia to the world heritage site of the underground rock churches of Lalibela.

It took several days on a bus to make it near to this area. Ethiopian roads, where they exist, still consist of tiny stones scattered over the reclaimed scrubland and the buses tend to move very fast. The texture of the majority of these roads is ribbed, like a thousand mini speed

bumps blended into their very fabric. This resulted in us spending day after day being shaken around like a NASA test pilot, and behind the bus a trail of dust blew up into the air giving any poor passer-by an unwanted dust bath.

With the insistent shaking of the bus, came the unfortunate re-occurring incident of the man who sat three rows in front of us. Above his small body were several large bags, which every few minutes would shake out of place and crash onto his head, to the amusement of many. The only foreigner we met was a Korean, who after a few days of travel on another bus, fell violently ill and spent a small fortune to hire a seat in a four-wheeled drive vehicle to exit the nation in comfort. It is possible for wealthy foreigners to visit these sites using a small aircraft, but that was not an option for us. Anyway, after all this travel the final destination proved itself worthy.

The rock churches of Lalibela are one of the wonders of the world. Built in the twelfth century, these eleven underground churches were cut out of solid rock and sunk fifty feet below the surface. It's estimated that the builders had to move 150,000 tons of rock over two decades to complete this project, and therefore we had to explore this labyrinth of tunnels and sealed mazes. This complex took us back in time to a lost age, locked inside Ethiopia and the priests inside claim to know where the original Ark is hidden.

In 1187 AD, the Islamic armies took Jerusalem and it soon became impossible for any Christian to make a pilgrimage to the city. In this context, Ethiopia's King Lalibela claimed he received a vision from God to build a new Jerusalem. Experts who have examined this complex suggest that in part, it was built like an underground fortress to protect these Christians from the threat of Islamic invasion, which did come later. As we walked down the steps and entered into the underground labyrinth of the Lalibela churches, we distinctly saw the chisel marks made by the labourers who only had primitive tools to use. This endeavour is unparalleled. We found many tunnels leading in every direction, some to the village and others to the water supply. In some areas, the tunnel system has not yet been opened and explored. In one part we were in complete darkness, until the light at the end of the tunnel pointed upwards to another church. Inside the priests were praying, chanting and carefully guarding the legacy of the Ark.

Within these churches we identified many Jewish and Christian symbols and some believe this could have been the perfect hiding place for the Ark of the Covenant; but now only a replica resides in each church. Yet, if we could examine a replica, we could learn if it meets the biblical criteria for the Ark. However the priests indicated this was not possible; for the Ark is too holy to be seen by outsiders.

Every Ethiopian Orthodox church contains a replica of the Ark of the Covenant in a part of their sanctuary which they call the Holy of Holies.

However, only the priests are allowed to go beyond the curtain to be near it. This veil separates the worshipper from the holy place and from a replica of the Ark. In every underground church, we found ourselves confronted with the veil, guaranteeing that no one could see a replica of their Ark. But suddenly we found a church where the curtain was left partially open and so I looked beyond the veil into their holiest place! Inside the Holy of Holies, I saw a rectangular container covered with a cloth being used as an altar. It was smaller than the biblical description of the Ark; there were no cherubim on top and the rings for

carrying it were absent. This was the closest we had been to Ethiopia's Ark of the Covenant, yet we couldn't get close enough to study it. We wanted to get near to the original Ark and the priests told us that the genuine Ark now resides in the sacred town of Axum. Our quest therefore continued onto this ancient site. What would we find?

A Lost African Civilisation
For Moses 'had married an Ethiopian woman' Numbers 12:1.

The Bible testifies that during periods in history Ethiopia played a role in biblical events; Ethiopians fought in some of the wars of the Bible and Moses married an Ethiopian. As we have already explained it is not possible to verify the actual borders of ancient Ethiopia for nations grow and contract, encompassing various people groups and lands. It may be the case that at times the land translated as Ethiopia in the Bible could be describing another people group in the region. Nevertheless the Scriptures do suggest that great kingdoms were located in this region and with this lead, we should be able to discover a substantial wealth of archaeological information in this land. After another bus journey we arrived in Axum and we soon began to find the relics of an ancient empire, fallen by the side of the road where it had collapsed

centuries before. Up until the twentieth century, few knew of this empire, except for brief vague references in antiquity and biblical records of a kingdom, Acts 8:27. Yet, by the hard work of archaeologists we began to uncover the lost Aksumite civilisation. Axum was once the capital of an empire which ruled this region from 400 B.C. until the tenth century. The most obvious legacy is the one hundred plus obelisks, most probably markers for the royal tombs of antiquity, which once contained outstanding riches of their age. In this obscure empire we found the largest monolith standing stone of the ancient world, which weighs up to five hundred tons and was cut from a single piece of stone. This nation had a language called Geez and they minted their own coins, which have been dug up as far away as India. These coins also provide archaeological data which give us a timeline for the religious shift from pagan worship to Christianity; for the pagan motif of a crescent was replaced with a cross. Our most important viewing was the Ezana Stone, a very large ancient memorial written in Greek, Sabaean (southern Arabian) and Geez. This is Ethiopia's Rosetta

Stone! This aged memorial immortalises the conversion of King Ezana to Christianity in the fourth century and dictates his victory over the biblical people of Kush. The Ezana Stone gives us empirical evidence for Ethiopia's transformation from pagan observance to Christianity in the fourth century and the Bible shows that some Jews began this process in the days of the apostles. To learn more about this civilisation, we began to examine ancient writings. *The Periplus of the Erythraean Sea* is a Greek manuscript which maps out the kingdoms on the Red Sea and beyond - Askum is mentioned. We also have a surviving letter from the Roman Emperor Constantius II to Axum, which indicates that

many Christian theologians began to be concerned that Ethiopia was straying from orthodox teaching. This letter is addressed to Ezana and asks for the head of the Ethiopian Church to visit Alexandria to contend about doctrinal errors which he held. Frumentius, their Syrian Christian leader probably never went and this appears to be the beginning of the separation of Ethiopian Christianity from the rest of the Christian world, and may be the birth of their hybrid Christianity, with its emphasis on the Ark of the Covenant. However, the evidence we have seen proves that a great civilisation was once in Axum, but nothing dates to the Queen of Sheba's time, when legend states the Ark arrived.

According to Ethiopian tradition, the son of the Queen of Sheba brought the Ark of the Covenant to this nation. Before we could establish if there was any veracity to this claim, we had to ask if there is any empirical evidence that she once ruled from this region. On the outskirts of Axum, we found the reconstructed remains of a large building, called by local legend the Queen of Sheba's Palace.

We studied the research into this ancient building and upon arrival Mathew's first point to me was that this complex is still very large by comparison to the huts many Ethiopians still live in. This signals that a very rich and powerful person once lived or ruled from this compound. The excavations in addition prove this is an old structure, but how old and does it date back to the time of Solomon and Sheba? At the present, nothing has been found in this area to prove that the Queen of

Sheba was once here, or that the Ark came to this nation. In any case, we spent some time with the German archaeologist directing this excavation, and he told us that they had dug deeper than ever before and his team claimed to have detected a level dating to the time of Solomon and

the Queen of Sheba. The chief archaeologist was very pleased to speak with us about his research and we exchanged details to follow up on his work. Most archaeologists still believe that a great deal of further study needs to be done in this structure before any final conclusions can be made.

We left this palace with no concrete evidence that the Queen of Sheba ever ruled in Axum and we could not find any artefacts that date to her age. The precise location of the Bible's Kingdom of Sheba is still a mystery. The Ethiopian book, called the *Kebra Nagast* contains the oldest claim that she ruled from this nation, but experts who have studied the text suggest it may only date to seven hundred years ago. This alludes to the possibility that King Ezana, with his questionable priest Frumentius, or one of their successors, devised the story of the Ark of the Covenant coming to the nation to solidify their theological and political positions.

On the famous Ezana Stone, one of the three texts engraved is the Sabaean language, and some experts have identified the similarity between the Kingdom of Saba and the recognition in the Hebrew language of the Kingdom of Sheba. The heart of this empire is found in modern Yemen, across the Red Sea from Ethiopia, and in her history, empires ruled parts of Eritrea and Ethiopia from Yemen. These people were famous traders and sold valuable items which the Queen of Sheba brought to Solomon and which were in use in Solomon's Temple, 1 Kings 10. Many of the archaeologists who have studied the question of Sheba's nation believe that discoveries made in Mareb, in Yemen, denote this is the most likely location for the Queen's Kingdom. The most convincing argument at present, is the presence of the glorified Bar'an Temple in Mareb, which indicates a wealthy kingdom existed in the land during the time of Solomon. By comparison nothing in Axum has been independently verified to date to this period. Also, monuments have been detected in the horn of Africa proving the Sabaean link.

With this new evidence available, we concluded that the legend of the Queen of Sheba may have been established in Ethiopia because of the authentic Sabaean presence in the land. Therefore, the case for the Ethiopian claim to have taken and cared for the original Ark of the Covenant is being weakened by this research. Yet, if we were to penetrate this story, we needed to be able to witness and examine the Ark itself, or at least a replica. Yet is it possible to get close to the Ethiopian Ark of the Covenant?

We have examined the case for the Ethiopian legend and we arrived at the monastery where the Ethiopians allege the Ark of the Covenant resides. At first, we walked around the modern church, where we saw another copy of the *Kebra Nagast* and we identified paintings that suggested how the Ark came to Ethiopia. One of these showed a priest carrying the Ark on his head and we immediately realised that this form of close association with the Ark was forbidden for the Levitical priests, 2 Samuel 6:6-17.

Afterwards we saw the ancient chronicles and manuscripts of this monastery, and the priests were especially interested in showing us the garments that were once worn in their ceremonies.

With our hearts stirring we walked towards the part of the complex where the priests state the original Ark of the Covenant is housed. We were informed beforehand that no-one gets to go beyond the blue gates, which separate the outer area from the inner section. Stationed by the gate was a guard, and we stopped by him and looked towards the church of the Ark. Then at the gate, we talked to one of the elders and he decided to give us permission to enter. We walked through and straight ahead we saw the home of the Ark. Just behind another set of blue gates and a blue curtain, the Ethiopians claim to possess the original Ark of the Covenant!

We were also given permission to go around to the other side of the building and for the first time we realised this was a two-story structure, giving the priest more room. We later found out that this space was very

important to him. We were told that the priest who guards the Ark has a very special privilege, and this honour comes at a cost. We asked if we could see the Ark, but we were told that only the chosen priest of this sacred sanctuary gets to be near the original Ark of the Covenant. The bricks that sealed the doorway on every side of the building are not just symbolic. Those who go beyond do so at the cost of

their lives; for the priest who gets this job is forbidden to leave the sanctuary and no-one else is allowed in. This tiny blue gate is the boundary over which the priest may never step. He is both the guardian of the Ark and its prisoner. His destiny is to die behind these gates and within the last few years, every priest who has received the role of the guardian has died within two years. Some of the priests are fearful and claim that the Ark itself is radiating some power which gradually kills them. I couldn't help think that the real reason for the high mortality rate was that elderly priests are the only ones entrusted with this special

role. We, like the priest in this photo, were locked outside of this sanctuary, so close yet so far. Just a few steps away from us the Ethiopian Ark of the Covenant is stored, but it was in every way out of reach. Was this a clever tactic designed to make it impossible to verify the Ethiopian claim to the Ark, or were the priests like Israel in fear of God's judgment on

those who misuse it? Beyond this fence the answers lie out of reach.

We found abundant evidence that these churches were built on ancient land, for the relics of the Aksumite Empire were buried everywhere. In addition, we saw ancient Christian monuments from a bygone age, woven into the very fabric of the new church buildings. In Axum, we saw proof of a Christian witness going back sixteen hundred years and we saw the forbidden home of the Ethiopian Ark. Yet, it seemed like our mission was ending without getting to see a replica of the Ark. We knew it would be impossible for us to see the original, but what about a copy? We then began asking around to learn if anyone knew where we could see a replica of the Ark. We were told this was most probably not possible, yet we could at least try at a small monastery at the highest point of Axum. Perhaps, if we were very fortunate the priests would allow us into the Holy of Holies to see a replica of the Ark. Would we at last succeed?

Using his zoom, Mathew took a photo of this church standing far off in the distance. We started to hike towards this high destination, crossing through various villages and like fire the news began to spread that foreigners were in the area. Three children came running towards us, with more coming after them. Before long we had a whole army of young people and children, who hoped we would take time out from our mission to throw a football around with them. When we complied with their requests a wave of laughter broke out and we continued on.

Then with a large crew, we crossed through this area and delved between various routes as the young people argued about the fastest pathway to the top. When we arrived at the gate on the other side of the hill, we found this was not just one church, but a monastery. One of the priests welcomed us in and led us to the storage facility where he brought out a selection of relics, from old crosses, to handwritten and elaborately decorated copies of various books of the Bible. Most of

our entourage

were bored and left us to go back to their homes. Then we began to take the last few steps towards the church on the hill, at the highest point of Axum. Leading us inside, the priest showed us some old Christian artwork and there was a small door that led into their holy place, where the Ark rested. We walked over to the Holy of Holies asking if we could enter and see the Ark's replica.

I cannot fully explain why, perhaps it was sheer desperation, but I hoped this priest would allow us through the veil to see the Ark. The church was deficient in size and just a few tantalising steps away the Ark was sitting, but the priest simply said, "No." It felt like we had travelled to the ends of the earth on our quest for the Ark and this was going to be the end of our endeavour! In a final futile attempt, I walked

around the back of the church, where a small opening ten feet above the ground allowed a little light into the Holy of Holies, and I placed our specialised one inch video camera extension into it. The viewer display revealed nothing more than a few flickers of light in a dark room. We then watched the sun go down and walked back down the valley to prepare to leave, and the sad realisation hit us that we would exit this nation without being able to see the Ark's replica. Suddenly something happened that changed everything. Mathew began to talk with a local man who reminded us that Ethiopia has a different calendar to the West and the following day was the beginning of their Easter celebrations, in which a replica of the Ark of the Covenant would be carried around town! So we

cancelled our plans to leave and awoke early the next day to finally see their Ark!

At four in the morning, we prepared for our long walk from the other side of town where we stayed to the monastery of the Ethiopian Ark. The streets were desolate and we hoped a vehicle would pass by in order to hitch a lift. We began to jog towards the monastery, until someone passed by and picked us up. The streets were still quiet and we wondered if the information we had received was correct. Would a replica of Ethiopia's Ark finally come out from their Holy of Holies? Then as we got closer, we began to see a few pilgrims appear from the side streets, dressed in white from head to toe. We felt a deep sense of relief that finally, after all this time we would get to see a replica of the Ethiopian Ark of the Covenant.

When we arrived outside of the monastery, we felt like strangers in an alien land. We were the only foreigners in a sea of Ethiopians, all dressed in white, holding candles. Then the people began to chant Christian songs. We had never heard anything like it before. It felt like we had stepped back in time to a civilisation that was bypassed by the modern world, where religious pilgrimage was still the central theme of one's life. Then suddenly, the moment we had waited for came as the priests emerged from the monastery carrying a replica of their Ark! Balancing the medium-sized rectangular box above his head, the priest put it on the central altar in town, which came from an ancient church. It was smaller than the Bible's description and it was covered in a dark red material; but we were glad to finally see it!

After about forty-five minutes of prayer and meditation, the chief priest took the Ark off the altar and placed it above his head. The men then began to walk in groups, followed by the women, with the Ark in the middle. As the pilgrimage around town started, a chant began at the front of the procession, leading in waves of sound all the way to the back. This chant always ended with the women and the sound of Ethiopian women singing or speaking is unlike any other we have ever heard. They are softly spoken, almost childlike. The sound is calming, gentle and friendly. We could liken it to a whisper or even a whimper. This was the sound that ended every section of praise to God. Then from the front, the chant would begin once again. We walked around town with the pilgrims and we could not use our camera flash, and our video camera had to be discreet.

We spent two hours in the presence of this Ark and we found a deep respect for the faith of these people. Yet we immediately recognised inconsistencies between the biblical description of the Ark and the Ethiopian Ark. It was the wrong size (Exodus 25:10-11, 37:1), the cherubims and the mercy seat were absent (Exodus 25:17-18); also the four rings on the sides and the poles for carrying it were omitted (Exodus 25:12-13). The greatest problem with the ceremony was the priests carried the Ark contrary to biblical law, which was a sin so grievous that it warranted immediate death (1 Samuel 6:19, 2 Sam. 6:6-9, 1 Chronicles 15:12-13). Another difficulty concerned the thousands of replicas of the Ethiopian Ark which have been made; in the Bible there was only one Temple where the Ark rested. In addition, the Ethiopian timeline is amiss, for the Bible states that the Ark was still in Jerusalem hundreds of years after the Ethiopians claimed to have taken it back to their nation (2 Chronicles 35:3).

Finally, we have the major problem of the theological argument for the use of the Ark of the Covenant within the Church. Now we must accept that theological persuasions do vary in the global Christian Church; in spite of this, there are some central doctrines that unite every believer in Christ Jesus. These doctrines are not to be found by studying the practices of any particular denomination, but can only be anchored in the teachings of the Bible itself. Before any doctrine is re-introduced into the worldwide Church, Christians have to ask themselves: Was this the doctrine of the early apostles? Is this what Paul, Peter and the disciples of the Lord taught? In other words, can we find this teaching in the biblical text and was this the religious observance of the first Christians in the New Testament? The Bible should be the source of all Christian practice, not tradition.

We must therefore start our evaluation of the Ethiopian tradition by considering the teaching of Jeremiah the prophet. Jeremiah was present in Jerusalem when the Babylonians destroyed Solomon's Temple and many years before, he prophesied that the Ark of the Covenant would lose its central role in true worship, and would not be made or visited anymore, Jeremiah 3:16. Within his lifetime, the Ark went missing and his prophecy was being fulfilled.

One of the major theological contentions this Church has is the error of practicing the idea of there being a 'veil' between God and man. The Church is divided, with the Holy of Holies being off-limits to God's people; but when Jesus died the veil in the Second Temple of Jerusalem was torn in two, Matthew 27:51, Mark 15:38, Luke 23:45. This indicates that those who put their faith in Christ's death and resurrection can now enter into the Holiest Place because of Jesus' perfect sacrifice. The Bible says we can 'enter the Presence beyond the veil' Hebrews 6:19. However, the Ethiopian Ark of the Covenant is still hidden and the way into their Holiest Place is still sealed. This contradicts the teaching of Hebrews 9, which confirms that the Ark of the Covenant and the layout of the Tabernacle was symbolic. 'The Holy Spirit indicating that the way into the Holiest of All was not yet manifest' Hebrews 9:8. We therefore learn that the divisions of the Tabernacle and Temple were designed to teach man that his sin has made it impossible for him to enter into God's holy presence, for 'all have sinned and fall short of the glory of God.'

This spiritual division was symbolically witnessed in the Tabernacle and Temple, where God's presence was always off-limits. When the veil in the Temple was torn in two, it bore witness to the fact that those who repent and put their faith in Christ's death and resurrection can have 'boldness to enter the Holiest by the blood of Jesus' Hebrews 10:19-20. The visible veil has been removed.

In the very early days of the Christian Church, the apostles had to discern if those who put their faith in Christ still had to fulfil the rituals of the Old Testament law. After much prayer, debate and testimony of God's blessings to the non-Jews, they agreed that Christians were freed from fulfilling Jewish customs, Acts 15. The law of the Old Testament was kept inside the Ark, but the New Testament reveals this law was a shadow of the good things to come in Christ, Hebrews 10:1. It was not the complete, but the forerunner. Christians should not look back to the Ark, but forward to Christ.

The Ark represented the promise that something better would come and Christ is the fulfilment of that promise. If we now try to put the Ark back into the central place of worship, it will take the emphasis off of Christ and set it onto a special object instead.

The two tablets of the Old Covenant were kept inside the Ark, but Christ's sacrifice created a New Covenant between God and man. The Apostle Paul was the most prolific teacher of the early Church and as an expert in Jewish law he also understood the transforming power of Christ's resurrection. The Ark of the Covenant was a sign of the separation between God and man, and inside the Ark was placed the law that no human was able to keep. The Ark reminded mankind of the impossibility of salvation. Nonetheless, the impossible requirements of the law were satisfied through the death of Christ. Paul wrote the law was our tutor which brought us to Christ, and only Jesus could fulfil and therefore abolish the law, Galatians 2:16, 3:24, Ephesians 2:15. Paul himself preached that those who believe in Christ's death and resurrection can be justified from all things, which could not be forgiven under the law of Moses, Acts 13:39. The impossible was now possible by faith.

Therefore Christians do not need a sacred box, hidden behind a veil, containing law. In Christ there is no veil. The law was fulfilled in Christ and only through faith in Him can we enter into His fulfilment.

It is true that the Bible locates some Jews in Ethiopia before the time of Christ and in 1983 modern Israel recognised the Jewish presence in the nation by airlifting some of them back to Israel, giving them citizenship. In Ethiopia, we found a deep respect for the sincere faith of the Orthodox Christians, though we had to conclude that their Ark of the Covenant did not meet the biblical requirements to be the original Ark of the Covenant. Therefore, if the Ark is not located in Ethiopia, where is it? Many scholars believe the Ark was destroyed by the Babylonians, for its gold was substantial and the wood was heavy and worthless to them. However, the Hebrews were meticulous bureaucrats keeping lengthy records of treasures lost and taken, yet in all the accounts there is no mention of the sacred Ark, 2 Kings 24:13-14, 2 Kings 25:8-17, 2 Chronicles 36:18-19, Ezra 1:7-10, Jeremiah 52:17-22, Daniel 5:1-3.

Over the centuries, many legends for the location of the Ark have been presented and most people find the wild claims too difficult to distinguish from the plausible. Therefore, we decided to study the other legends of the Ark, to examine the genuine possibilities and more importantly to disregard those which have no credibility.

Legends of the Ark are established on many foundations; some are ancient writings, others are biblical clues and a few are based on myths, dreams and highly charged imaginations. Experts call the latter pseudoarchaeology. This includes archaeological excavations, publications and 'artefacts' which disregard accepted archaeological methodology, do not conform to standard data collecting techniques, and refuse to accept examination, and critiques from professional archaeologists. It is obviously evident that many scholars differ on numerous interpretations of the meaning of artefacts retrieved from antiquity and concerning their dating; yet scholars should agree on the accepted methods of excavations, and data should always be available to those who wish to test any claim or discovery.

For example, in 2003 an artefact appeared in Israel called the Jehoash Inscription, with an ancient Hebrew engraving including the name 'Solomon.' This would have been the first time the name of the Bible's

Solomon had been found; however the discovery of this relic was hazy, it lacked authenticated provenance, the owner was secretive and doubts were raised. After a thorough investigation, it was revealed that an intelligent man had forged the inscription and had scammed the experts through tedious research. On the other hand, the Tel Dan Stele, which is inscribed with the 'House of David' was found by an excellent archaeologist, giving us a precise location of the discovery and an exact excavation layer. This signifies that we can trust this antiquity and confirm its date. Knowing the exact location of the discovery is as important as the interpretation of the artefact. With this in mind, pottery is of absolute importance in the dating and excavation of archaeological layers; for its uniformity helps to determine the age of discoveries from antiquity.

As broadcasters and authors, it was expedient for us to be able to distinguish between genuine skilled archaeological discoveries and pseudoarchaeology, which have no credibility. Experts disagree on the meaning of discoveries from antiquity, but they should not disagree on the professionalism of excavations.

In this inquiry, our mission involves broadcasting the artefacts that have been found and evaluating the meaning of them in the light of expert opinion. Clearly we are not involved in the task of excavation, for our job is to examine all the theories, ideas and published work of experts, and to deliver a broad presentation. Only by evaluating the entire body of work can we come to meaningful conclusions. We have to consider every angle, and ask why archaeologists came to their conclusions and why other experts contest them. In this light, we believe we are able to see the larger picture, rather than just one opinion, which may be abstract, distant or contended.

As mentioned in earlier chapters, there are often two ways for people to examine the Bible and archaeological discoveries. The first is to stress what has not been found, the other is to shed light on what has been found. The secular media usually approaches the Bible focusing on what has not been detected and quickly overlooks what has been; this leads to doubt. However, after spending time to study what has been retrieved, we learn that a substantial body of evidence has already been recovered to confirm the accuracy of Scripture. Many theories have disputed the authority of the Bible, yet when new finds vanquished these, they rarely get press. Also, we have many unique biblical finds, but the legends get the publicity!

The Knights Templar
'Even those from afar shall come and build the Temple of the Lord' Zechariah 6:15.

The Templar Knights existed for approximately two centuries during the Middle Ages. They were considered to be the Special Forces of the Crusader period, for their skilled fighting units and expertise. As European Knights their mission was to serve and protect pilgrims to the Holy Land, originally gaining little for themselves. In 1129, they were officially endorsed by the Roman Catholic Church and they helped free the Holy Land from Islamic rule, setting up their base in Jerusalem on the sacred Temple Mount. This order of Knights made pilgrimages safe for Christians to visit the Holy Land and operated a medieval banking fund, allowing a pilgrim to put money into a 'Templar Bank' in London and withdraw it in the Middle East. With the charges on these exchanges and the glory earned for their skills, the Templar Knights became wealthy, and spent their riches building churches around Europe, and Castles in the Middle East. During this period, the Knights Templar had full access to the Temple Mount, where Solomon's Temple once stood. Consequently, some have claimed that this order excavated on the Temple Mount and found the golden treasures of Solomon, including the Ark of the Covenant and smuggled them back into Europe, to hide them all beneath various churches in France, England and Scotland etc.

However, this powerful order, which was once the hero of all Europe, fell out of favour with the King of France and their secret initiation ceremonies led to mistrust and accusations. Many were tortured into confirming charges made against them and in 1312, the Pope dissolved them. The rapid disbanding of the premier European organisation of their age and the transfer of their wealth into other hands, led to the proposal that their treasures were spirited away and hidden in various churches, never to be seen again.

The Temple Church in London was built in the late 12th century by the Knights Templar as their English headquarters. Designed to resemble the Church of the Holy Sepulchre in Jerusalem, it is now famous for the effigy tombs, where Knights lay in wait for the resurrection. This church featured in *The Da Vinci Code*. Rosslyn Chapel in Scotland also appeared in the book and the facts about it remind us that this book is fiction, for the chapel was built a century and a half after the dissolution of the Knights Templar. Historians also confirm that the family who built the chapel testified against the Templar Knights when they were on trial. The crypt of this chapel has been sealed for many years, allowing imaginations to project fantasies that the Holy Grail, the Templar Treasures or the Ark may be in a subterranean vault, below the secret stairway.

Those who search after the treasures of the Knights Templar follow clue after clue, from stained glass windows, architectural mysteries, to ancient images. This quest for the treasure of the Templar Knights has more in common with Hollywood, than history. The Knights Templar continues to inspire imaginations because they are regularly portrayed in books, on TV, films and in computer games. When a rich and powerful organisation suddenly falls and its wealth vanishes, the unanswered questions left behind remain to tantalise subsequent generations. Over the centuries, facts and myth intertwine and legend begins. Nevertheless, in the modern era new investigations propose that the financial problems of the King of France made the dissolution of the Templar Knights a convenient act, which helped solved many of France's problems.

Some have alleged that these Knights found the chambers of the first and second Temples in Jerusalem. However, archaeologists have been able to excavate many of the Templar Knights locations, and are able to give us a proposal of how much they achieved in their search. In Jerusalem itself, many tunnels and chambers have been uncovered, which appear to have been unopened since the time of Christ and if Solomon's treasures had been retrieved, they would have been paraded about, as was the case with many other 'relics' which the Templar's possessed. Yet, the question of the depth of the Temple Mount evacuation remains unanswered.

In the 1930s during British rule in Jerusalem, the director of the British Mandate Antiquities Department carried out the only official archaeological excavation under the Al-Aqsa Mosque, on the Temple Mount. R.W. Hamilton's photo archive of this project shows a Byzantine mosaic floor underneath the mosque, suggesting it was built on the site of a church / monastery. The exact penetration of the Templar Knights on the Temple Mount is open to speculation, but with excavation forbidden, it appears little more will be known until the situation changes. At the present time, the evidence suggests that the only secret treasure that the Templar Knights bereft to this generation is the unending treasure of the imagination.

Parker's Dome of the Rock Excavation
'They have taken treasure and precious things'
Ezekiel 22:25.

I found a copy of several newspaper pages dating back one hundred years ago, whose headlines state: 'Fear Diggers took Ark of the Covenant,' 'Gone with Treasures that was Solomon's' and 'Have Englishmen found the Ark of the Covenant?' Jerusalem was in uproar, rioters were mobbing the streets and the Dome of the Rock was immediately shut. On the run were several members of the 1909-11 Parker Expedition, which had received official permits to excavate in the land, but who in desperation had illegally entered the Dome of the Rock to dig. A century later, I stumbled upon these forgotten reports in my research.

The newspapers read like a movie script, containing reports that Solomon's wealth may have been found and stolen. The leader of the expedition was Captain Montague Parker, who had raised a great deal of money, worth millions today, based on the conviction that Valter H. Juvelius had detected a Bible code in Ezekiel's book. This code could only be understood in ancient Hebrew and to them it revealed the whereabouts of the Temple treasures. The prophet Ezekiel witnessed first hand the fall of Judea to the Babylonians and he lived to become a Babylonian captive, where the Ark may have gone. Based upon new discoveries in Jerusalem and Juvelius' Bible code, a new theory was proposed, and the explorers drew up maps, sketches and clues to assist them, along with archaeological finds.

Just forty years before, British archaeologist Charles Warren had found a complex of tunnels in the Holy Land and with Jerusalem's unknown tunnels being rediscovered the Parker Expedition believed they could uncover the lost Jewish treasure. In 1909, they arrived in Jerusalem with a permit, but were not allowed on the Mount itself.

They began to excavate by the Gihon Spring, six hundred metres to the south of the Mount, laboriously clearing Hezekiah's Tunnel and other labyrinths. The Parker team found themselves in the tunnel that the Bible's King Hezekiah had ordered to be made, before 701 B.C. 'It was Hezekiah who blocked the upper outlet of the Gihon Spring and channelled the water down to the west side of the City of David' 2 Chronicles 32:30. 'As for the other events of Hezekiah's reign, all his achievements and how he made the pool and the tunnel by which he brought water into the city...' 2 Kings 20:20. This tunnel is another proof of the Bible's accuracy in its description of ancient history.

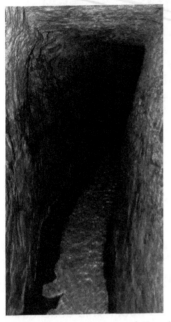

Controversy soon arose that not one member of the team was a professional archaeologist and it was alleged they had inexhaustible funds in order to bribe the locals. As the years passed, they penetrated labyrinths underground, but they were still too far away from the Temple Mount. Pressure mounted on the team, as the financial backers began to demand results, just at the same time the permit to excavate from the Turks was ending. What would they do?

In a desperate attempt, Parker's team bribed the locals, wore Arab clothes and secretly entered the Temple Mount digging in the southeast corner of Solomon's Stables. Still with no success, on the fateful night of 17 April 1911, the excavators entered the Dome of the Rock, having made a deal with the Muslim in charge and began lowering themselves into the cavern inside. Reports later suggested the men had smashed through rock to find a shaft below, but their noise was heard and a Muslim attendant cried out to raise an alarm. The team quickly fled, fearing for their lives at worst, their freedom at best. In the chaos of the next few days, rumours spread that the Ark of the Covenant, Solomon's Crown and other precious artefacts had been stolen. In fact, Parker and his team escaped out of the region empty handed on a boat, never to return.

One hundred years later these press reports still inspire an Indiana Jones moment, but in truth, they are a perfect example of how secrecy, misinformation, speculation and the media's desire to get attention can create myth. The Parker Expedition had sought relics for profit; it ended with a quick exit, no artefacts and the investors losing their money. Nevertheless, the drawings of the excavation of the tunnel still serve us and visitors to Israel can enter this tunnel oblivious to the reason why it was excavated in secrecy.

Mount Nebo, located in western Jordon, is 2,680 feet above sea level and on a clear day Jerusalem can be seen from the top. It was on this mountain that the Bible states Moses went to view the Promised Land, Deuteronomy 34:1. Mount Nebo is also famed as the resting place for the Ark of the Covenant. The apocryphal book of 2 Maccabees 2:4-7, claims the following account of Jeremiah: 'The prophet being warned of God, commanded the Tabernacle and the Ark to accompany him, as he went forth into the mountain, where Moses climbed up (Mount Nebo) and saw the inheritance of God.' He 'found a hollow cave, wherein he laid the Tabernacle and the Ark and the altar of incense, and so stopped the door. Then some of those that followed him came up to mark the place, but they could not find it.' The book then suggests that Jeremiah was angry with these people for trying to record the location and told them, "The place shall be unknown until the time that God gathers His people again together and receives them unto mercy."

The book itself dates to around 190 B.C. and may have been written by rebel Jews in Alexandria, Egypt. It surfaced many centuries after the time of Jeremiah and was rejected by the Jews as non-historical, and not inspired by God. Protestants follow in the tradition of the Jews, stating the book is neither historical, nor inspired and state its contents contradict the teaching of Scripture. The apostles in their letters never quoted from it. Scholars believe the first book of Maccabees contains some historical value, but the second is mostly fiction, with little to offer. This imaginary story of Jeremiah hiding the Ark and other items is also out of sync with history, for the prophecy stated these objects would have been found and returned to God's people when the Lord gathered, 'His people again together,' which happened when the ancient Jews returned from Babylon.

Nonetheless, these facts have not dissuaded people to hunt for the Ark on this mountain and in 1981 an American explorer claimed to have found the Ark in Mount Nebo; he even took an illusive photo which I was able to track down. The length of this 'Ark' is 62 inches long, and its height and width are both 37 inches. A strip of wood went around the edges of the Ark, with one in the centre dividing the main wooden panels in half. The pattern on the lining appeared as tiny flowers and the two divided panels at the front were engraved with a criss-cross pattern. This box was covered in brass, not gold. One archaeologist who studied this case established that the photo proved undeniably that this Ark was made with modern materials, which can only be sourced today. This claim sunk as fast as it had arisen and even conspiracy hunters are relatively calm about it. The story of this find was exciting to read, nevertheless it is interesting to note that many 'finds' of the Ark all came about at the same time as Hollywood's Indiana Jones retrieved it! Like many other accounts of people finding the Ark, this man also made claims to Noah's Ark, the Tower of Babel and others. His discovery was also aligned to a prophecy that he gave in the 1980s, in which he would become one of the 144,000 described in the outline of the end times in Revelation 14:1, and that the return of Christ would take place in the 1980s. He never explained why he didn't find any of the other biblical articles that were also 'hidden by Jeremiah.'

With the excitement of the discovery of the Dead Sea Scrolls, numerous caves in this region have been excavated, but there is no sign of the Ark. It is also important to remember that Jeremiah was considered as an enemy of the Levites because of his prophecies of the fall of Judah. The Levites were the only people who had access to the Ark and they would not have allowed him to take it away. Secondly, it would be impossible for Jeremiah to have been able to hide the Ark before the Babylonians came, for the Bible states that he was in prison, Jeremiah 37-39. This falsified story of 'Jeremiah' is not historical, it is not inspired and its claims contradict Scripture.

Jerusalem's Secret Temple Chamber
'I will give you the treasures of darkness and hidden riches of secret places' Isaiah 45:3.

The Bible meticulously records the fate of the Temple treasures, yet it never details the loss of the Ark. Why is this? When this question is put to leading Rabbis they often smile and declare, "The lost Ark of the Covenant was never lost at all!" According to this Jewish legend, a secret chamber was made under Solomon's Temple and it was this chamber that kept the Ark safe from Pharaoh Shishak, and all the other invasions of Jerusalem. Some date the chamber to the time of Solomon, others to Josiah. This theory suggests the Levites in accordance with emergency protocol, placed the Ark into the sealed chamber when the Babylonians invaded and it was never retrieved because the Jews were never truly independent, until now.

The Wailing Wall in Jerusalem is the holiest place for Jews. Thirty years ago, two leading Rabbis who were responsible for the Wall, became so convinced of the secret chamber account, that they began an illegal excavation under the Temple Mount to find it and the original Ark within! After many months of digging, they claimed to have broken through into an unknown tunnel, which was sealed for thousands of years. However, after eighteen months of digging and clearing, their secret excavation was discovered and the Israeli authorities under great pressure stopped the dig, and the Muslim authority on the Temple Mount protested until it was sealed. The Ark which felt so near was still out of reach.

There have been many claims to have located a 'secret resting place for the Ark,' yet this account is the only one situated below the site of the two Jewish Temples. It is held by the ancestors of those who served in the Temple and has been propagated by the most senior Rabbis in Israel. These excavators were not discredited adventurers, but revered spiritual leaders and the descendants of the keepers of the Ark. In addition, archaeologists have proved that the Temple Mount contains many tunnels, which are now illegal to excavate. With these facts, it is possible for many to take a leap of faith to suggest one of these may lead to a secret chamber. Testing this theory however, may not only lead to the Ark, but also to attempts to destroy the Dome of the Rock, the beginnings of the building of a new Jewish Temple and a Third World War!

- 155 -

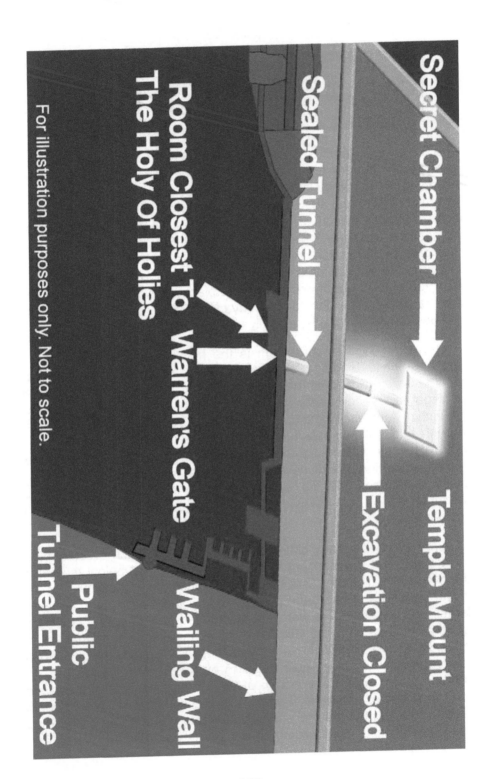

Secret Chamber ➡

Temple Mount

Sealed Tunnel ➡

Excavation Closed

Room Closest To **Warren's Gate**
The Holy Of Holies

Public
Tunnel Entrance

Wailing Wall

For illustration purposes only. Not to scale.

St. John's Revelation of the Heavenly Ark
'The Temple of God was opened in heaven and the Ark of His Covenant was seen in His Temple'
Revelation 11:19.

Those who believe the Ark of the Covenant is locked inside a chamber under the Temple Mount state that it was never retrieved in antiquity, because the dominating threat from foreign powers such as Babylon, Persia, Greece and Rome never ceased. The memory of each invasion became so severe in the Jewish psyche that fear of losing the sacred Ark guaranteed its seclusion under the Temple. This fear was compensated in 63 B.C., as Rome's Pompey conquered Jerusalem and forced his way into the Holy of Holies. Inside he was puzzled to find an empty space. A hundred years later, the Temple was in ruins and the Jews scattered. Over 1,800 years passed and in 1948, Israel's rebirth gave hope that the Ark could be retrieved.

In that time the mystery of the Ark has captured many imaginations and now according to some leading Rabbis, the true hinderance to finding the Ark of the Covenant is not knowing where to search, but getting permission to search. Many people have alleged to have seen the Ark or solved the mystery, and in our investigation we have travelled far, explored many lands and studied these claims. Some stories fall apart after a little research; others take time to dig very deep to find the truth. Now at the end of our investigation we have concluded that only two cases for the Ark still stand. The first is that the Babylonians destroyed the Ark, burning the wood to get the gold. The problem with this theory is that the two tablets of stone, which recorded the covenant between God and Israel, would have been useless to the Babylonians, and the ancient Jews would have risked everything to save them for posterity. This never happened. The second theory is that the Ark now rests inside a secret chamber below the Temple Mount in Jerusalem, Israel. The problem with this theory is its impossibility to test, for any attempt to excavate below the Mount always leads to unrest, protests, violence and may even trigger a global war starting with Islamic nations invading Israel.

In the hunt for the ancient treasures of the Bible, the sacred text gives us a detailed account of what was once possessed by the Jews and where most of it went. Enormous amounts of wealth were spent on building the Jewish Temples and making the relics that went into them.

These items were in turn plundered by Egypt, Syria, Assyria, Arabia, Babylon, Sidon, Tyre, Philistia, Greece and Rome. The monuments of Egypt and Rome prove this loss, as well as the chronicle of the historian Josephus. Yet in the end, the Bible itself indicates that the treasures of the ancient Jews were fleeting.

In the first century, the Jews were still hoping that a Messiah would come and deliver their nation, so they could worship freely. When Christ began to teach, His chief concern was for the souls of men, rather than establishing a wealthy Jewish Kingdom with fleeting riches and temporary treasures. When the disciples stood amazed at the Temple, He prophesied its destruction. To a rich young ruler He said, "Give all to the poor and come follow Me!" In the Temple Jesus overturned the tables of money changers and used a whip to clear it of those who sought profit instead of prayer. Finally His sermons asked penetrating questions concerning the fragility of the soul. In one parable he spoke of a rich man who stored up wealth to live a life of pleasure when God said, "You fool! This very night your soul will be required of you." Jesus challenged those who came to Him and spoke of eternity, hell and the judgment to come asking, "What will a man give in exchange for his soul?"

Treasure hunters still seek the Ark of the Covenant and many claims have been made and continue to be made. Perhaps Jeremiah's prophecy of 3:16 was the final word on the Ark; or maybe John 3:16 was the final word for those who hope to see the Ark once again. The Bible states: 'For God so loved the world that He gave His only begotten Son, that whoever believes in Him should not perish, but have everlasting life.' This time, the precious gift from God was not the design of a golden box, but His only Son. The Apostle John witnessed the life of Christ and in the last days of his life, he saw a vision of Christ in heaven and of the Ark. The Bible itself reveals that eternal life is not a right to be demanded, but a gift to be received by faith. The apostles preached that all need to repent, and put their faith in the death and resurrection of the Lord Jesus Christ, Acts 2:31-40, 13:28-39, Romans 10:8-13. Those who repent and believe the gospel will by faith receive all the mercy obtained by the sacrifice of Jesus on the cross. In addition, the book of Revelation indicates that those who put their faith in Christ may one day get to see the heavenly Ark, in the eternal bliss of their spiritual home. 'God will wipe away every tear from their eyes, there shall be no more death, nor sorrow, nor crying. There shall be no more pain, for the former things have passed away' Revelation 21:4.

ByFaith Media DVDs

If you enjoyed the search for the Ark of the Covenant and the exodus evidence, you can also watch these investigations on your TV!

ByFaith - Quest for the Ark of the Covenant contains four episodes.

Episode 1: Tutankhamun's Treasure and the Ark of the Covenant.

Episode 2: Pharaoh Shishak and the Gold of Solomon's Temple.

Episode 3: Jerusalem's Wealth and the Lost Jewish Temple.

Episode 4: A Forgotten Civilisation and the Ark's Legacy.

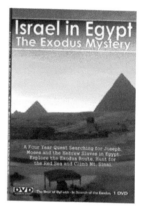

You can also join the brothers Paul and Mathew on their investigation to find the evidence for the Bible's exodus. **Israel in Egypt, the Exodus Mystery** DVD is now available. Find out more at www.ByFaith.org.

ByFaith - World Mission DVD. Join Paul and Mathew as their mission expeditions take them into 14 nations. 85 minutes.

Great Christian Revivals on 1 DVD is an uplifting account of some of the greatest revivals in Church history. Filmed on location across Britain and drawing upon archive information, the stories of the Welsh Revival (1904-1905), the Hebridean Revival (1949-1952) and the Evangelical Revival (1739-1791) are told in this 72-minute documentary.

Visit **www.ByFaith.org** for trailers.

Samuel Rees Howells: A Life of Intercession by Richard Maton. Learn how intercession and prayer changed history.

Samuel, Son and Successor of Rees Howells by Richard Maton. Discover the full biography of Samuel Rees Howells.

The Holy Spirit in a Man by R.B. Watchman. An autobiography.

Tares and Weeds in your Church: Trouble & Deception in God's House by R.B. Watchman.

How Christianity Made the Modern World by Paul Backholer.

Holy Spirit Power: Knowing the Voice, Guidance and Person of the Holy Spirit by Paul Backholer.

Heaven: A Journey to Paradise and the Heavenly City by Paul Backholer.

Jesus Today, Daily Devotional: 100 Days with Jesus Christ by Paul Backholer.

Britain, A Christian Country by Paul Backholer.

Celtic Christianity and the First Christian Kings in Britain by Paul Backholer.

The Baptism of Fire, Personal Revival and the Anointing for Supernatural Living by Paul Backholer.

Glimpses of Glory, Revelations in the Realms of God by Paul Backholer

The End Times: A Journey Through the Last Days. The Book of Revelation...by Paul Backholer.

Debt Time Bomb! Debt Mountains: The Financial Crisis and its Toxic Legacy by Paul Backholer. Ebook.

Notes

Notes

Notes

Lightning Source UK Ltd.
Milton Keynes UK
UKHW021110150822
407314UK00006B/97